SOUL EXERCISES FOR THE OPEN MIND

A Psychic Development Workbook
A companion book to
Open the Mind Exercise the Soul

Featuring "The Psychic Minute"

JOHN CAPPELLO

BALBOA.
PRESS
A DIVISION OF HAY HOUSE

Balboa Press books may be ordered through booksellers or by contacting:

Balboa Press
A Division of Hay House
1663 Liberty Drive
Bloomington, IN 47403
www.balboapress.com
1 (877) 407-4847

Because of the dynamic nature of the Internet, any web addresses or links contained in this book may have changed since publication and may no longer be valid. The views expressed in this work are solely those of the author and do not necessarily reflect the views of the publisher, and the publisher hereby disclaims any responsibility for them.

The author of this book does not dispense medical advice or prescribe the use of any technique as a form of treatment for physical, emotional, or medical problems without the advice of a physician, either directly or indirectly. The intent of the author is only to offer information of a general nature to help you in your quest for emotional and spiritual well-being. In the event you use any of the information in this book for yourself, which is your constitutional right, the author and the publisher assume no responsibility for your actions.

Any people depicted in stock imagery provided by Thinkstock are models, and such images are being used for illustrative purposes only.
Certain stock imagery © Thinkstock.

ISBN: 978-1-5043-4413-5 (sc)
ISBN: 978-1-5043-4414-2 (e)

Print information available on the last page.

Balboa Press rev. date: 1/6/2016

TABLE OF CONTENTS

DEDICATION

This book is dedicated to the memory of Russell Alldredge from Abilene, Texas.

PREFACE

With today's society changing at an ever faster pace, there is a need to recognize our psychic abilities and develop tools in order to manage them. Many people are finding that they need to learn more about themselves and their personal abilities in order to live in today's world. They need to give themselves permission to be more human. We have learned that human beings are equally physical and spiritual beings, and this fact is causing many people to evaluate the way they care for both their physical and spiritual natures.

As mankind's physical well-being continues to improve with advancements in medicine and technology, better physical health allows us to explore and push our human experience to new limits. It is giving us the opportunity to focus our attention in other areas, allowing us to grow and discover more about our spiritual reality. We are learning that we can develop methods for our soul to grow in ways we have not considered in the past.

Our spiritual growth is often maintained by being associated with a religion, philosophy, or an ideology we find fulfilling. We find comfort in them, and there is no shortage of people promoting different points of view. There are times, however, when we find our comfort level in a chosen area is not enough to satisfy our need to learn more about ourselves. Furthermore, we realize that there is more to our spiritual nature and that exploring the limits of it does not conflict with most belief systems. This book is about observations and the self-empowerment in an area whose time has come.

So…let's begin.

INTRODUCTION

I am John Cappello, and I have been interested in metaphysics since I was a child and have worked as a professional in this field since 1997. My journey in discovering my abilities began in earnest after the death of my father in 1992. This workbook is a reflection of my experiences and study of my own abilities. It is intended to give a foundation to students wanting to have a grounded approach to understanding *their* abilities.

Throughout the workbook, there are various bullet points I call "Psychic Minutes" and exercises to assist you in examining your soul's experiences. Listed throughout each chapter, the soul exercises and exams are there to help you recognize and pay attention to your soul's energy. The psychic minutes are definitions, soul exercises and/or meditation points to consider. They are designed to be short, distinct encapsulations of thinking points for you, the reader. There are sixty psychic minutes for you to remember. They are re-enforcements about the time being *now* for you to acknowledge your abilities.

The "hour" of psychic minutes can be daily affirmations or areas to think about during your day. They are reminders of this ability we all have but do not fully utilize. They are a start for your new journey. It is up to you to maintain and finish the journey based on your will to move forward with the lifestyle of a practicing psychic. This lifestyle can be private, and it is suggested that your abilities not be used to set you apart or be used as a tool to build your ego. There is a responsibility and humility to the work. It is your moment of decision. It is your *hour* that has come.

Soul Exercises for the Open Mind is a companion workbook to the book, Open the Mind Exercise the Soul, and a textbook for use when taking the first series of psychic development workshops offered by me and my company, the Visionary Workshop, LLC. The series is designed to assist you in developing your psychic abilities and give you a foundation for understanding them. It will attempt to disprove myths about this talent and give you a comfort level that you will be able to take with you for the rest of your life. There are many approaches that may be used to develop your skills, and I suggest you investigate the ones that appear to be legitimate and helpful to you.

To enhance your natural abilities, learn to trust your impressions and learn to understand the way things work with you. This workbook does not explore the use of tools such as tarot cards, the pendulum or other divination techniques, as depending on them is not our focus. There is nothing wrong with using tools, but once you learn about your personal skills, you may find that they get in the way of your abilities. That being said, they can still be used effectively to validate your impressions if you experience doubt. If you have an interest in one of them, there are many books available that focus solely on specific tools. The information you learn will supplement the work you do with this workbook.

Being a psychic and using your soul's energy as part of your everyday life is natural, but it takes practice and a willingness to accept the improbable. It is an 'art' and a life style choice that I will discuss over and over again during this book. There is a kind of science associated with this work as well. Our brains and our bodies play a major part in our ability to sense information because our bodies work with our soul's energy, and being psychic is one of our soul's qualities.

I wish you the very best on your endeavor and hope you enjoy this book that was created with the best of intentions!

CHAPTER ONE

FOUNDATIONS

The bright neon sign of a hand outside the building said, "Psychic". The nearby sign said, "Open".

Psychic ability remains one of the greatest gifts given to mankind from the Divine, but the image that many people have come to associate with it is negative. A neon sign on a building does not mean that the people inside are unscrupulous, but it is an image that often represents a view that the general public has of people who use their gifts. It is unfortunate since this is a natural talent that all of us possess to some degree. This image is a result of the exploitation of vulnerable people in their time of need. An example that comes to mind is a man who was once told that he had a 'curse' on him, and that he had 'come to the right place' to have that curse removed… for a price! This sort of exchange is damaging to people and damaging to the reputable people in the profession. It is the case that the few who abuse are the ones who get the publicity.

A person using any type of talent or ability has an obligation to use their gifts genuinely and for the greater well-being of the client. A psychic is no different and has the responsibility to work ethically, with a high sense of integrity. The wonderful and mysterious ability of the human soul to capture information needs discussion and rational tools to recognize when these special mechanisms are activated. We explore gaining access to your wonderful and mysterious abilities.

This workbook is about developing your soul's psychic abilities and using them appropriately, for the general good. It is about self-empowerment. Before you proceed, you should ask yourself a few questions. Why am I interested in learning to use my psychic abilities? Why do I want to start this Psychic Journey? What do I want to learn about myself so that I can understand others? The answers lie in your own personal experiences, disposition, and ethical background. There are no definitive methods to developing the mechanics of psychic abilities, but there are similarities within all of us that can help us relate. We will be exploring these similarities while allowing you to have your own unique talents surface. These talents should be nurtured and developed. They are part of learning to use your soul's energy as a tool for understanding life's challenges.

You will need to determine your unique profile and decide how you will use your talents. We will start working on your profile right away in this first chapter. First, lose all of your preconceived notions of psychics and their abilities. This will allow you to have a fresh start.

It is very important to be yourself and allow your abilities to flourish unimpeded with ideas, techniques, or philosophies that will not serve you. If you follow the top psychics and mediums in the United States, you will notice one common theme with all of them. They are being themselves and do not do anything extraordinary to connect with their abilities. They have learned to trust their gifts and not to question their validity, and they trust the information their soul has acquired for them to interpret. This is a key element in your personal development. You must learn to trust yourself!

Please note that psychic ability comes from the information gathered by your human soul. The Divine makes the information available, but you have to learn to accept it and then use it properly. We are ultimately spiritual beings with a body, and our souls are immortal. It should be no surprise that your soul is an integral part of your information gathering as a human being.

Like any other area of study, the art of being a psychic means there are a few areas that should be recognized. And because it is an art, some will be better at it than others. There are definitions, different techniques, and a language used to acquire information by the psychic. The language of the psychic is simple but succinct. It is "I feel," "I see," "I hear," I know," "I smell," or "I taste." The definitions are sometimes individual because we are all unique, but for the purpose of this workbook, we will be using "Psychic Minutes" to explain the way things work in this field. The techniques or tools are not like those used in any other profession because they involve using the energy of your soul. It is the use, familiarity, and trust of the energy around you that will give you an edge in understanding information being gained by your soul. The journey of learning is fascinating, rewarding, and troubling all at the same time.

Dwelling on particular impressions can affect you physically. You need to remain detached so that you do not absorb negative energies. For example, if you choose to work with crimes or find that you sense illnesses, you will need to be careful. These energies will weigh you down. It is necessary to pull away from negativity and take care of yourself when you are a psychic. Many people who work with negative energy find that they need to comfort themselves with food, drink, or even sex in some cases. These activities are normal, but relying on them to extreme levels can be unhealthy in the long run.

Sensitive people are those who are razor sharp in determining the meaning of subtle energies around them. They must learn to be in control of their emotions when working with energies outside of themselves. They can be fooled at times, but more often than not, they can be "dead on" in recognizing with great accuracy the details of a situation. While analyzing energy that is bombarding them, a psychic may appear to be very meek. However, this is far from the truth. It is the focus on the energy instead of their physical surroundings that accounts for this appearance of eccentricity and disorientation.

This book is divided up into soul exercises and a series of "Psychic Minutes" to help you define the process as you go along. Psychic Minutes are not just definitions but tips that I have learned over the years to help you recognize your talents. It is important work to learn about psychic ability, and one day it will receive the proper recognition that it deserves. You can play a part in making these abilities more credible by being yourself and using your talents for good.

The first psychic minute, about exercising the soul's energy, offers an explanation of the way the soul gathers information. It answers the most obvious question that you may have about this book. "How do you exercise your soul?"

Psychic Minute One

We exercise our souls by examining our past experiences, paying attention to sensations and impressions from beyond the physical, and practicing.

This basic observation sets the tone for your development and the use of this book. I will continually ask you to observe with your senses beyond your physical senses because this is where the energy of the soul functions as a mechanism for psychic ability. It is the portion of the soul that exists beyond your body that we concentrate our efforts. This area is where you are sensitive to the unknown, outside yourself. The concept of interpreting and becoming skilled in recognizing the powerful energies around you leads us to the next psychic minute.

Psychic Minute Two

The energy of your soul captures energy from the Divine and sends energy that can be interpreted.

Imagine the energy of your soul being like a rubber band ball with virtually unlimited rubber bands surrounding a center. These rubber bands represent events in a person's life, and when one of these rubber bands or a life event is stressed, it separates itself from the others in the ball. As an individual band, detached from the ball, it enters the orbs of another person's soul energy. When this happens, the band becomes energy that is readily readable by another person.

These energies may cross, run parallel, or line up exactly to the reader's energy. Energies striking each other create fragments of information for the reader, bands that run parallel allow the reader to see the edges of the person's life, and when the bands line up with the reader's energy, the information comes to them something like a movie. Furthermore, they may come through any of our psychic senses; feeling, seeing, hearing, smelling, tasting, or knowing.

THE WORKBOOK

This workbook allows you to explore the energy of your soul and gives you tools to use to discuss it. Before we begin though, you will want to understand the language and terminology used to discuss your impressions. The language is not highly technical but is necessary to help comprehend the elements of the work. You will learn that there is a mechanism within our souls that enables us to be what we call, psychic!

We will be discussing different terms throughout this workbook, but the basic ones are simply about feeling, touching, seeing, hearing, smelling, tasting and knowing. Over the years, many words and phrases have been coined to describe these senses. The following are terms which are often used interchangeably:

Psychic feeling, clairsentience, clairempathy

Psychic touch, psychometry, clairtangency

Psychic sight, psychic vision, clairvoyance

Psychic hearing, clairaudience

Psychic smell, clairfragrance, clairolfactory, clairscent, clairaroma

Psychic taste, clairgustance, clairgustus

Psychic knowing, psychic thoughts, claircognizance, intuition

Whether or not you realize it, your psychic abilities are extensions of your physical senses. We use them interchangeably with our physical senses, and they work together in a kind of symphony. They make us unique individuals in the universe because our abilities are more developed than other creatures. There may be others more developed, but they have not made themselves very evident so far.

I believe we have three types of senses that we work with on an ongoing basis. Our physical senses, our extended senses, and our remote extended senses. The extended senses are the ones we know to be the psychic senses. The idea that we have a "sixth sense" is not accurate from my perspective because it limits the true nature of the soul that has many ways of sensing information. It is just one myth that exists about psychic ability.

You will find that many people are very dismissive of psychic ability and are extremely skeptical of those who embrace these gifts. Most skeptics fall into one of the following categories: they do not accept their own abilities, they have misconceptions about psychic abilities, they are in denial, or they want to exert a kind of control over other people. To each his own, but you should not be deterred if you want to explore your own abilities and gifts. They are human, natural, and good.

Many people say they are not psychic and have never had a psychic experience. These people are the ones who may dismiss a "first impression", a "hunch", or another sudden idea they received and could not readily explain. I want you to notice I used the term "received" in my last sentence. It will be important as we start our journey.

There is a simple test for those who believe they are not psychic, and it is an event most of us have experienced. Have you ever had someone get into your "personal space"? That is, has someone gotten so close to you that you felt a little violated? If so, then you are noticing your soul's energy. You want people to back away from you when they are not invited to be that close. It is a sensation that we usually remember about another person because it is just a little traumatic.

Once you understand this uncomfortable moment, you might use it to start building your psychic profile. Those who say they have never had a psychic moment might recall an instance when they sensed a little violation of their space. If they are being honest, they should acknowledge that their senses exist beyond their physical presence. They were not actually touched. They did not see anything out of the ordinary or hear anything, but something just wasn't right. They had a "sense", but it wasn't physical.

Sincerity is important on both sides of the psychic communication. The psychic must act with integrity, and the client must be as honest as possible when accepting information. This work is the easiest of all to disclaim because it must be acknowledged or verified before it can be claimed. When a person does not give validation to accurate information, it can cause the psychic individual to lose confidence and be reluctant to use their gifts for others. This is an area of concern of which I hope you will be aware and not allow it to deter you in your development. Just like other professions, psychics have a range of capability and vary in personality. In general, an accomplished psychic will have a range of accuracy of 80 to 100 percent depending on their abilities.

Psychic information is the energy of the moment, and energy changes. For this reason, predicting the future can be unreliable at times. We have freedom of choice and can use that freedom to make a new future. The choices of others may also change the future. The most stable energy is that of the past and can therefore be read with the highest level of accuracy.

VALUE OF BEING A PSYCHIC

Why should we learn to be psychic? This question can be answered simply by saying, "It allows us to grow." We gain insight and perspective, and it inspires us to create. Furthermore, we learn about the strengths and weaknesses of our personalities. The human soul is our consciousness, and its perspective is stretched. It tests our value system and teaches us about the valid points of view of other people. Finally, learning to use and trust our intuition and other abilities can assist us in a time of need.

Psychic Minute Three

Psychic ability allows you 1) to have an early warning system to prevent you from being in danger, 2) validates or does not validate impressions you receive from your physical senses, 3) gives perspective, and 4) allows you to create. It is the energy of inspiration!

GETTING STARTED

We will begin our journey by learning a little bit about you. Do you just feel things that are going to happen? Do you see, hear, or just know the solution to a problem? Do you smell a fragrance or have a particular taste in your mouth, providing insight about a situation? The answers to these questions are important because they are indications about the strongest skills you possess. I believe that analyzing your impressions is your first step to understanding the way your abilities work. We are all a little different, and the way you interpret information is unique and very special.

Psychic Minute Four

The way you understand your innate abilities helps you learn about your strongest psychic skill.

Soul Exercise

Write down in 25 words or less a time you did the following:

I felt this about

_____

I had a vision of this

_____

I heard about this

_____

I just knew this about

_____

I sensed a fragrance about

_____

I sensed a flavor associated with

_____

You will be asked these questions again, but I wanted you to start your quest to be a psychic with a small self-quiz. I think you will find this book is going to make you work! It will make you think, and you might just have some fun as well.

Since much of society continues to have issues with psychics, those of us who practice our abilities are taking a risk. However, you will learn that tapping into your psychic abilities will give you a new perspective on life. It will allow you to understand others better and possibly anticipate the future. All the while, you will be enriched and learn more about who you are and this makes the work you are about to do priceless.

Learning to be psychic means that you must understand that it takes discipline to harness your talent. It took me many years to learn about my skills, and I continue to explore the limits of my ability. I have learned that psychic ability has specific rules to it that you can follow.

These rules allow you to accept the unexplainable and broaden your awareness about the human experience. It is amazing the way we can capture information, but we often are not able to interpret it. I hope you will keep this workbook and look at it from time to time. You may understand more and more each time you read it. Keeping an open mind, practice, and experience allows a psychic to become more accurate.

Psychic Minute Five

There are two sides of psychic energy. The energies of sending and receiving energy are equal.
We emit energy from our soul/bodies, and it can be read. Our emotions and the events in our lives have specific energy that we understand, and the energy we send is *received* by others.

- Sending Energy—The sending side, when it comes from the psychic's perspective, involves telepathy, telekinesis, and healing. Reiki and other modalities involving healing are techniques the psychic uses when helping others by *sending* healing energy. It can be argued that these modalities use both sending and receiving energy, but they are for separate discussion. This workbook can only scratch the surface of interpreting energy that has been received and does not attempt to cover the first side of sending energy to others, *masculine* energy.
- Receiving Energy—Receiving energy is natural, but we often do not interpret the messages accurately. It is amazing that energy can be in the form of discernable information. The human soul is the force around us that is able to interpret information and does this in many ways. Through definitions, examples, and exercises, we will assist you in learning the way your soul captures information. This is *feminine* energy. It is with this in mind that we move to our next Psychic Minute.

Psychic Minute Six

Practice and validation are important assets to have when learning to use your abilities.
It is suggested you find a willing partner who you do not know very well to help you with your development. A like-minded person will be honest with you and allow you to scrutinize their work skills. When this is not possible, you will have to use another tool to evaluate your progress. An alternative is journaling. This important tool will help you with your confidence and evaluate your strengths and weaknesses as a psychic.

Psychic Minute Seven

A journal chronicling experiences will help you with your psychic profile and validate your skills.
The soul exercises in this workbook can serve as the beginning of a journal that you can tailor make to your own needs and personality. I recommend journaling as a practice to

record your personal observations and as a way to express yourself. It is not only a tool for development but therapeutic as well.

Your physical senses are an integral part in the development of your psychic senses. And while psychic and physical abilities are used in conjunction with one another, you need to learn to use the psychic senses independently. This workbook will help you explore the singular use of these "extended" senses and allow you to experience the full power of your soul's energy.

ACCESSING YOUR SENSES

There are two ways to access your psychic ability. The first one is meditation. When you meditate to develop your skills, you first set an intention. You are giving your soul permission to access information from beyond the physical. For example, an intention might be, "What is the best career for me?" One meditation may not be enough, but it allows your soul to access the answer you seek. You will learn what information is psychic versus imagination or mind clutter based on the way the information is received. The psychic impressions are the ones which are sudden and unpredictable.

The second method is to quickly interpret impressions we receive in everyday life such as sudden feelings, visions, sounds, smells, tastes, and knowing. This workbook is designed to give you the opportunity to use your psychic abilities in real-world situations without the need to always be in a meditative state, and that is our focus. Your soul's energy is always available to capture information that must be interpreted quickly. This is why you should learn to pay attention to the signals your soul gives you during your everyday life. However, since learning to trust and let go of your logical mind is essential for you to develop, a brief meditation will be at the end of each chapter to help you learn to trust your psychic abilities. Quietening the mind is essential to develop a high level of accuracy.

When you meditate, remember to set aside a specific period of time just for you and the four tenants of meditation. The first is to find a comfortable place that is quiet and serene. The second is to start to relax and focus on your breathing. The third is to clear your mind, and the fourth is to rest and allow information to come to you. We will be discussing meditation in more detail in the next chapter.

Soul Meditation #1

If you wish, use recorded music to help you relax. Start to notice your personal space around you. Clear your mind and let go of thoughts and emotions. Once you are relaxed, begin to set your intention. Send out to the universe your desire to learn to use your natural abilities to do positive work in the world and prosper with your gifts. Ask to develop your extended senses of feeling, seeing, hearing, smell, taste and knowing.

Once you have spent time meditating on each of the psychic senses, you should thank the universe for your gifts and begin to feel energy moving back into your body. When you feel fully energized, you can end your meditation and resume your daily activities. Use your journal to record your experience.

Soul Exam

Have you ever been aware of information that you knew originated from another dimension?

_____

Do you have preconceived ideas about psychics and mediums?

_____

Have you ever received information suddenly and recognized it?

_____

Do you have confidence in your psychic abilities?

_____

Do you have an interest in face readings and understanding body language?

_____

You should develop your psychic skills using tools that enhance your physical senses. Techniques such as face reading, learning to read body language, and handwriting analysis are useful tools to help activate your psychic abilities. Practice is essential. With repetition, you will become more comfortable and confident with the energy that you are able to receive and interpret. You will also become more aware of how the psychic senses work for you. We always suggest that you observe other psychics, receive readings, and practice giving readings. We will be exploring methods to use your naturally strong senses and help you enhance those that are either not strong or not existent at this time.

THE DEVELOPMENT PROCESS

Developing your psychic skills requires *paying attention* to impressions you receive and recognizing the meaning of those impressions. We learn to use physical experiences to help us when we have a psychic moment, and practice allows you to learn about observing with your psychic or "extended senses." Meditation helps you by creating an environment that "deprives" your physical senses and gives your psychic senses the opportunity to be fully used without influence.

In addition to the previous methods we have discussed, remember that we have said to observe other psychics, get readings to gauge their accuracy, and give readings to others. By observing other psychics when they are working, you will learn from them. Notice the way they are accessing their abilities and begin relating their techniques to your own abilities.

Receive readings to learn the way a client will feel when you are giving a reading. Receiving a reading will also help you to measure the accuracy of the psychic giving you an assessment. Finally, give readings to others and let them critique you. You will begin to understand that the way you say things can be pivotal in gaining the trust of your client. The more accurate your language to your client, the better you can describe an event you sensed. This may be some of the best advice given to you throughout this book!

FINAL THOUGHTS

Balance in your own life is important if you are to be a practicing psychic. A self-absorbed person or one with a lot of mind clutter will not do well working with energy. Psychics who talk about themselves or drift off-topic usually do so because their personal lives are in chaos. Keep in mind that we are providing an important service to others, and they should be our focus.

The following chapters will continue to explain each of the psychic abilities in greater detail and will challenge you to work with your soul's energy. We must first, however, continue to create a foundation on which you can build. This foundation will serve you well for the rest of your life or as long as you continue to inquire about this wonderful gift that most of us do not use to its fullest capacity.

CHAPTER REVIEW

In this section, it is important to demonstrate that you are retaining the important elements of this chapter. Quiz yourself about the Psychic Minutes and make them part of your knowledge base of psychic information. This will prove invaluable to you once people begin asking you questions, trying to gain an understanding of your beliefs in psychic abilities. Some of this quiz is just about stretching your memory and recognizing where you are on your psychic journey.

On a separate sheet of paper answer the following questions:

1. Where does psychic ability come from?
2. What is an example of using the language of a psychic?
3. What is the value of using psychic ability?
4. What are the two types of psychic energy?
5. How do you use your physical senses to aid you in developing your psychic skills?

CHAPTER TWO

INTEREST IN METAPHYSICS

Metaphysics and *New Age* are two of the common terms associated with the community of people who practice using their psychic talents, and the interest in the philosophy of metaphysics or "the study of existence beyond the physical" continues to grow. You are part of this growth, and you will be part of bringing psychic ability out into the open. It is no longer acceptable to keep these talents "hidden" or consider them to be part of the occult. They are only hidden or unacceptable in the minds of those unwilling to acknowledge them and view them as a part of our journey in this life.

Psychic ability from the soul validates that there is existence beyond what our physical senses identify, but there is pressure to dismiss and discount unexplained phenomena by many. One of the challenges of learning about your psychic abilities is to obtain support from people around you. It is important to surround yourself with like-minded individuals who are open to unexplained experiences. A healthy concern about truth and honesty is good, but if you are around those who are not "believers", then you may become frustrated, stop acknowledging your experiences, or stop talking about them altogether. Skepticism is good to a point, but your psychic journey must allow you to persevere until you become successful in learning the way your abilities work with you.

The best psychics are skeptical people, but they are open-minded to possibilities. They recognize their own abilities and admire others who are not afraid to express themselves. Psychics understand that energy is only accurate in the "moment" and can change quickly. A good psychic is someone who does not appreciate someone only trying to act a part. They can usually spot a fake in an instant. Skeptical psychics are not cynics. They are people who are open to more than just their own opinions and abilities!

Our society sends conflicting signals to people who say they are psychic, and this just means there is confusion about this area. The evidence of the existence of psychic ability may not be measurable by instruments at this time, but in the future it may be possible. How do you measure the energy of the human soul? Research continues to be done, and the work is becoming further legitimized by the ever increasing number of people who are investigating their own experiences.

It is important to stay positive and not be discouraged when developing your skills. You probably have had experiences that you could not explain with your logical mind that caused you to want to investigate further. However, the hesitation to proceed is normal. At one extreme, there are the tricksters who claim to have abilities that prove to be phony. At the other extreme, there are those who are so negative that they refuse to acknowledge the possibility of the unexplained. This is when you must have faith in yourself and know that the impressions you receive are real. You must learn to acknowledge the energy of your soul.

Studying psychic ability means that you are open minded and allows you to join those who must have scientific evidence of the gift. It does not deny you the opportunity to research its validity. The Skeptic Society is one of these organizations who claim to be open minded if empirical evidence is shown to them. Their website describes their philosophy as follows:

> *"The Skeptic Society is a nonprofit 501(c)(3) scientific and educational organization whose mission is to engage leading experts in investigating the paranormal, fringe science, pseudoscience, and extraordinary claims of all kinds, promote critical thinking, and serve as an educational tool for those seeking a sound scientific viewpoint. Our contributors—leading scientists, scholars, investigative journalists, historians, professors and teachers—are top experts in their fields. It is our hope that our efforts go a long way in promoting critical thinking and lifelong inquisitiveness in all individuals."*
>
> *"It is the application of reason to any and all ideas — no sacred cows allowed. In other words, skepticism is a method, not a position. Ideally, skeptics do not go into an investigation closed to the possibility that a phenomenon might be real or that a claim might be true. When we say we are "skeptical," we mean that we must see compelling evidence before we believe."*
>
> *For more information about the Skeptical Society, go to their website <u>www. Skeptic.com</u>.*

Proof of psychic ability is the validation of the sensed energy, but it may only be the validation of the moment. It is subject to the interpretation of the receiver and may prove to be wrong after logical inspection. This is the truth, and that is why it is difficult to codify techniques and have hard fast undeniable rules. If you had a proven "formula" for psychic development, it would take away from your freedom of choice and deny you the opportunity to change your situation in life. Everyone would win the lottery, and there would be no chances in life! The wonder of living would no longer exist, and we do not want that to happen.

This reality does not lessen the value of psychic ability. It means that it allows you another tool to help you make decisions and grow. We are sensitive to others and compassionate because we can understand other perspectives and learn from them. Psychic ability is there to enhance our lives and make us better spiritual beings. It can improve our relationships and make us well-rounded individuals.

In the previous chapter, I asked you to examine your experiences and determine your psychic profile. The personal exam should have been revealing to you about your abilities and served to indicate your strengths and areas of potential improvements. In this chapter, you should begin to examine the reasons why you are drawn to learning about psychic ability and metaphysics. It will be revealing to understand yourself and the reason you want to be more sensitive to the world around you.

Psychic Minute Eight

Most people are drawn to metaphysics through a trauma, an event, or a curiosity that causes them to examine their belief systems and/or explore their personal abilities.

The types of traumas or events in a person's life include: the death of a friend or loved one, a divorce, an illness, a near death experience, financial distress, etc. These events are often "life altering" and cause one to begin re-evaluating his or her core values. The core values of the person are tested, and those values or beliefs that withstand these tests will remain. The values that now fail will either be abandoned or modified to suit the person's altered needs.

When a person suffers from a trauma, it can be both physical and spiritual. The physical wounds may heal perfectly, but the ones the soul encounters may last a lifetime or never heal completely. A person who is violated may never fully recover from the event. It alters their perspective and can inadvertently cause them to recognize their psychic abilities. It is their soul's energy that they are recognizing and giving more of their attention. This "awakening" can be a very enriching opportunity to those who accept it.

In my case, it was the death of my father that piqued my curiosity to explore my abilities and metaphysics. The idea that my father was attempting to communicate with me by appearing in one of the buildings he owned caused me to investigate. I met several people in the profession and asked their advice to verify the phenomena to the best of their abilities. I found their work with me to be interesting, and I decided to learn more about my own abilities.

The experience with my father was an eye opener. It was a first-hand experience of something I could not easily explain, and I was a skeptic. My thoughts and training did not allow me to accept the possibility of a paranormal experience. It did not fit my practical 'left brain' education. I have a degree in Economics and a Master of Business Administration in Management.

Soul Exercise

What trauma, event, or other reason led me to be drawn to metaphysics?

_____

_____

I found the episode with my father led me to the next Psychic Minute.

Psychic Minute Nine

The study of metaphysics and/or psychic ability by individuals is a "journey of self-discovery".

13

I watched the psychics and mediums I consulted regarding my father and noticed that they were very sensitive to impressions they received from the energy around them. They took nothing for granted and had open minds about the information they received. It was astonishing that they knew personal facts about my father, much of which they had no way of knowing.

The mind of an MBA is impressed when the perception of having a leg up or an advantage in business is available. It is important to be flexible and willing to learn new things, in my opinion, so it is not a stretch to want to know, "How did you do that?" Skepticism falls away when you cannot dispute an undeniable reality. This is the spot in which I found myself.

I decided to take classes to determine whether or not I had any psychic abilities. I discovered that I had to tune into myself and learn how I received information. I had to take time to meditate and begin to accept information. Trusting the information was the next hurdle I had to overcome. I had to learn about me before I could move forward working with my ability.

Soul Exercise

What have you learned about yourself that makes you want to explore metaphysics and/or your psychic abilities?

_____

_____

At this point, it is important to take a moment to start defining metaphysics and psychic abilities.

Psychic Minute Ten

Metaphysics is the study of existence "beyond the physical".

The study of metaphysics was introduced by the Greek philosopher, Aristotle. He defined the term, metaphysics, and caused Western philosophical thought to consider the existence of 'being'. The knowledge of a reality beyond the physical senses is accepted because it is recognized that there is light our eyes cannot see, sounds we cannot hear, and energies affecting us that we do not completely understand.

Animals routinely see, hear, or sense energies which we cannot with our physical senses. We solicit them to assist us in many ways such as the use of specially trained dogs to find people or drugs. Observing animals has given us clues to existence beyond the physical.

Science is discovering methods of proving the existence of many 'energies' we have not been able to sense on our own. Technology has us understanding new dimensions and exploring areas never dreamed of in our human history. The problem with our science and our technology is that it still has a long way to go before it is able to quantify and identify psychic ability.

Aristotle defined metaphysics, but he did not explore the reality of mankind's human ability to access information beyond the physical. He did not recognize psychic ability. This ability has always been a part of our humanity, but it is often maligned and treated as if it is imagination.

Soul Exercise

How have you discovered reality beyond the physical in your life?

_____

_____

We have stated that psychic ability is the soul's capacity to capture information beyond the physical limitations of the senses. Defining psychic ability is essential if we are going to understand the phenomena. Also being described as a metaphysical ability, psychic ability suffers from a range of criticism from scientists, religious organizations, and skeptics in general because of the intangible nature of its existence. The reality is that everyone has the ability to some degree, but it is misunderstood. It is the information received from energy, and the interpretation of that information that is subject to debate.

Accuracy and relevancy of information ranges from worthless to priceless, and this determination is subjective. There are no 'right or wrong' answers because information is simply received and discerned. The use of psychic abilities is a practice and needs to be understood in this manner.

A person in the psychic field can be trained by attending schools and workshops dedicated to the development of ability, but until there are more established and recognized rules, it will not receive the respect it deserves from the skeptical community. Practicing psychics and other individuals have a range of ability.

The range of ability is defined as the percent of accuracy in discerning information as well as the area of psychic sensitivity. Individuals can have from virtually zero to over 90 percent accuracy in their ability to discern information. The testing of a range of abilities is difficult due to a lack of a complete understanding of the sense. Over a period of time through testing and research, standards will be developed for psychic ability.

Soul Exercise

How do you experience your psychic ability?

_____

_____

Soul Meditation #2 – Reviewing Your Personal Belief Systems

In this meditation, you will begin to examine your belief in psychic abilities and search within to learn the origins of your philosophies of life.

Begin by going to your peaceful or sacred space where you start to relax and focus on your breathing. As you are relaxing, the rhythm of your breathing becomes deeper and deeper. Your mind begins to clear of all of the worries and cares of the day. This is when you are able to reflect upon your core beliefs and discover your personal comfort level with exploring your psychic abilities. You may find you are modifying or changing your beliefs in order to allow yourself to move forward. It is important to always respect other belief systems and accept that others may not believe in the same things that you do. This is, however, your journey, and you must seek your own truths in your life. Meditate on these thoughts for as long as you wish.

Once you have allowed your conscience to be satisfied with moving forward, you begin to feel energy come back into your body, and you can resume your normal activities. This session will be one to reflect upon in the future as you continue to grow and expand your belief system. Because your intent is good, you should be comfortable with knowing this work is good and wholesome.

Chapter Review

On a separate sheet of paper answer the following questions:

1. What validates existence beyond the physical?
2. What is the skeptic society?
3. What are some examples of life changing traumas that often cause an interest in metaphysics?
4. What is psychic minute nine? How does it relate to you?
5. What is metaphysics?

CHAPTER THREE

YOUR PSYCHIC PROFILE

In the first chapter, we discussed your psychic profile. We will now begin a deeper understanding of each psychic sense and how your abilities work with you. By this time, you should be aware of the different sensations that are associated with each psychic sense, and we will continue to review and practice using them in this chapter. Your memory will continue to be fertile ground for you to determine your psychic strengths, but we can now start to look further within and practice with more purpose.

Psychic Minute Eleven

Developing psychic skills involves discovering a personal profile of abilities.

These abilities include psychic feelings (clairsentience), psychic touch (psychometry, clairtangency), psychic visions (clairvoyance), psychic hearing (clairaudience), psychic smell (clairfragrance), psychic taste (clarigustance), and psychic knowing (intuition, claircognizance). Each of these abilities is present with most people; however, there is usually one that is more prominent than the others. Some people are equally strong in several areas, but generally, one sense opens the door for other senses to be noticed. Your soul has sensitivities associated with these psychic terms. They are akin to muscles in the body but are energy areas that can be strengthened with practice.

You can learn about each of your abilities by self-examination. In order to determine which senses you are most inclined to use, you need to ask yourself questions about each area of psychic abilities. Here are some examples of the types of questions used when making a personal assessment. Please note that there is no right or wrong answer to any of the following areas of inquiry.

Soul Examination #1—Psychic Feelings (Clairsentience)

1. Do you have sudden feelings about people or situations without any provocation?
2. Do you often feel drained or nauseous or have headaches or other physical sensations after being in a crowd?

3. Do you have emotional first impressions about individuals or situations?
4. Do you find you are often alone because you have to recharge your energy?
5. Do you often say, "I just felt I knew the answer?"
6. Do your emotions allow you to have visions, hear solutions to issues, or just know answers to problems?
7. State a typical emotional experience you could not explain.

Soul Examination #2—Psychic Touch (Psychometry or Clairtangency)

1. Do you ever walk into a room and feel that negative or positive energy was there?
2. Have you ever held an object from another person and felt you knew information about them?
3. Are you able to identify emotions from a person's voice when they are attempting to disguise their emotions?
4. Have you ever changed furniture in a room and felt that the energy in the room changed?
5. Do you ever purchase items simply because they have good energy? Do you pass on items because you feel bad energy?

Soul Examination #3—Psychic Vision (Clairvoyance)

1. Do you have sudden flashes of images of a future event?
2. Do you have vivid prophetic dreams? (This means that your dreams come true.)
3. Do you have experiences of déjà vu?
4. Do you "visualize" events in your mind? Do you say that you "saw" the solution?
5. Do sudden images in your mind create emotions, allow you to hear words or phrases that answer questions, or allow you to solve dilemmas?
6. Describe a sudden vision of a future event that gave you reason to believe you have clairvoyance.

Soul Examination #4—Psychic Hearing (Clairaudience)

1. Do you just hear words of encouragement or warning about a person or situation?
2. Do you hear the name of a color like yellow, red, blue, etc… around a person? (These are the colors of auras and have meaning.)
3. Do you hear words that serve as "mantras" for you?
4. Do you have first impressions by hearing words about a person or situation?
5. Do you hear words that come to you, without provocation, that solve a problem?
6. Do you notice you say that you "heard" the answer to a problem?

7. Do you hear words that allow you to sense an emotion, see a vision, or just know the answer to a question?
8. Can you recount a situation when you heard a voice or words that prompted you to believe that you have the gift of psychic hearing?

Soul Examination #5—Psychic Smell (Clairfragrance)

1. Do you ever notice odors prior to encountering a person or situation?
2. Do you form first impressions based on a non-physical odor?
3. Do you notice that odors come to you to help you solve problems?
4. Do you notice odors that allow you to sense an emotion, see a vision, or just know the answer to a question?

Soul Examination #6—Psychic Taste (Clairgustance)

1. Can you recount a situation when you noticed a taste in your mouth that allowed you to believe that you have the gift of psychic taste?
2. Do you ever suddenly taste flavors when you encounter certain people or situations?

Soul Examination #7—Psychic Knowing (Intuition or Claircognizance)

1. Can you recall a time when you followed your intuition and had successful results?
2. Can you recall a time when you did not follow your intuition and wish you had?

Compiling Your Data

Using the self-examinations above, please assign each sense a percentage from 0 to 100% based on your strengths in each area, totaling 100%.

_____ Psychic Feeling
_____ Psychic Touch
_____ Psychic Vision
_____ Psychic Hearing
_____ Psychic Smell
_____ Psychic Taste
_____ Psychic Knowing
100% Total

This is a good starting point to evaluate your strengths. Practice and observing your own behavior will allow you to judge your talents with more accuracy. Each of these abilities will be discussed in detail later in the workbook.

Soul Practice- Start Learning About Your Personal Psychic Profile

An examination of previous experiences will allow you to gain an understanding of your own talent as a psychic. You will learn about the areas of your soul associated with these psychic skills. Consider at least ten experiences or impressions you have had in the following areas: 1) precognition, 2) validation or lack of validation of your physical senses, 3) experiences when you gained perspective or solved a problem, and 4) experiences when you created something that was totally original, such as a song or a new way to do an activity. Ask yourself about those experiences, and in the space below or in your journal, write them down under the four different categories: Precognition, Sensory Validation, Perception Adjustments, and Creativity/Innovation. As you are remembering each incident, be sure to begin by writing down the sensation you had when the impression first came to you. You might say, "I felt this," or "I had a vision," or "A voice in my head said to do this," for example. Continue asking those questions when you are considering things you just "knew," "smelled," or "tasted" when there were no physical stimuli to create those sensations.

It may take some time to recollect so many experiences, but it is worth it to spend some time in reflection. Once you are satisfied with the number of experiences you have written down in each of the areas, you can begin to calculate your results based on the categories.

Precognition

Write down precognitive incidents you have had in your life. These experiences allowed you to avoid a potentially difficult situation.

1. _____
2. _____
3. _____
4. _____
5. _____
6. _____
7. _____
8. _____
9. _____
10. _____

Sensory Validation

Write down impressions that validated feelings you had about a person or situation. These experiences may be first impressions, past events, or present situations around a person.

1. _____
2. _____
3. _____
4. _____
5. _____
6. _____
7. _____
8. _____
9. _____
10. _____

Perception Adjustments

Write down experiences, sudden or unexpected, that gave perspective about a situation.

1. _____
2. _____
3. _____
4. _____
5. _____
6. _____
7. _____
8. _____
9. _____
10. _____

Creativity/Innovation

Write down times when you were suddenly inspired with a totally original idea, created a song, or just solved a perplexing problem.

1. _____
2. _____
3. _____
4. _____
5. _____
6. _____
7. _____

8. _____

9. _____

10. _____

Write down positive and negative experiences. Psychic experiences are neither good nor bad, but they can help you determine the best course of action to take when you are facing difficult situations. Repeat this exercise several times. There may be some sensations that you have never experienced or cannot recall. This is okay. When you are satisfied with your answers, move the next category.

Recognize the number of times you wrote "I felt, I saw, I heard, I knew, I smelled, or I tasted" a sensation when the energy was captured by your soul. Divide the total number into each sense, and you will understand that you are stronger in certain senses than others, or you are evenly divided between them.

After you have finished with the categories, you will need to add up the total number of experiences that you have written down and determine the sense with which you tend to capture the most energy. Recognize, for example, that if you had 100 experiences and 60 of them were feelings, then you are 60 percent a psychic feeler. The other senses are percentages less than this one, but they still may be present to some extent.

Psychic Minute Twelve

We access our psychic abilities by using "extensions" of our physical senses.

Physical Sense	Location on body	Psychic Sense
Touch	Skin	Clairtangency
Sight	Above the eyes	Clairvoyance
Hearing	Above the ears	Clairaudience
Taste	Mouth	Clairgustance
Smell	Outside the nose	Clairfragrance
Knowing	Above the head	Claircognizance
Feelings	Chest and stomach	Clairsentience

*Note: These senses are the most common. Mediumship and Channeling are advanced skills to be covered with other Psychic Minutes.

Identifying the senses and their locations is just the beginning of your development. Your soul's energy corresponds with the areas of your body that is associated with each of the psychic abilities. Once you understand that your soul and your body are psychic tools which you can use to capture information beyond the physical, you can move forward. The area of your body associated with each sense provides insight and understanding. This knowledge will help you when the area "just beyond" the physical area is activated. You are energy, and when your energy is disrupted by a different energy, you can sense it and identify it. However, it takes meditation, practice, and patience with each area.

Soul Exercise

What information have you received in each of these areas in your life, if any?

Please answer this question by listing the senses and reviewing your Psychic experiences:

Psychic Sense   Experience

_____   _____

_____   _____

_____   _____

_____   _____

_____   _____

The following three things will help strengthen your understanding of how you capture energy: the identification of the physical senses, the areas where you access your psychic abilities, and their names. This knowledge is helpful, but it still does not give you a mechanism to use these abilities. The mechanisms you will use develop over time, but the foundation of your development starts with meditation.

Psychic Minute Thirteen

The primary mechanism to access your psychic abilities is meditation.

When you start accessing your abilities, you need to learn to clear your mind and let go of your thoughts and emotions. Once you are clear, you can start noticing energy around you. Learning about meditation is a key to this process.

Meditating is easy, safe, and creates a healthier lifestyle. The benefits of meditating are far reaching, affecting your physical and spiritual well-being. Making a commitment to meditation will open up your awareness to your talents, and it only takes a few minutes to get started.

1. Make time in your schedule for quiet time.
2. Find a quiet, comfortable place to sit.
3. Once you are relaxed, start allowing your mind to quiet and rest.

During your meditation, you can use a recorded meditation or music to help you relax. Once you are relaxed, start to notice your personal space around you. Your personal space is that area where you would feel uncomfortable if someone entered it uninvited. An example is when someone you don't know well stands too close to you. The awareness of your personal space is the next key element in developing your psychic abilities as we will be using this space as a tool. Once you have identified it, I want you to explore it with your feelings. Exploring this space may be uncomfortable but necessary for you to grow.

Soul Exercise

What do you notice about your personal space as you meditate?

_____

_____

The discovery of meditation can be life altering. It is a door opener for your psychic abilities, and it is time to start exploring them. The tool of meditation and noticing your personal space creates the foundation for our next Psychic Minute.

Psychic Minute Fourteen

Clairsentience is the soul's capacity to capture "feelings" or emotional information beyond the physical limitations of the nervous system.

Clairsentience or psychic feelings are often called the first psychic sense because most people use this sense more than any other. Our emotions make us unique and are easily accessible. Emotions are part of our humanness.

We notice our psychic feelings (emotions) in common situations such as first impressions, hunches, and gut feelings, and we have the ability to study and understand them. However, whether or not we act upon them is another issue. Often, we ignore or dismiss these sudden unexplained feelings. They are not taken seriously because there is no logic associated with them. These impressions may not make sense until a situation unfolds, and the information is validated. Once our feelings are validated, we find ourselves questioning why we did not accept them at first. This acceptance often can save us time, effort, and aggravation.

When we have these sudden feelings, the personal space around us is activated. For some people, the entire body can be affected with a feeling, but recognizing it can be difficult without some practice. For when we are not practiced, the feeling may only be recognized later, after it cannot change the outcome of a situation.

You can practice using your clairsentience is by doing the following:

1. Meditate and clear your mind and emotions.
2. Recognize your personal space.
3. Dwell on various feelings and take an "inventory" of them.
4. Observe and pay attention to the effect of dwelling on those emotions.

Observing and paying attention to your emotions will give you clues about information you receive outside of meditation. The safe place of meditation will allow you to practice pushing out your personal space and expanding your field of sensitivity. Pushing out your personal space is like casting a net of energy seeking other energy to sense.

The energy emitted by another person can be sensed by your energy net. Once you are confident about the energy you are sensing, you can judge with your feelings about a situation. Learning to trust and discern is the most difficult part of learning about this psychic sense.

Soul Exercise

What emotions have you recognized and feel confident sensing from another person?

_____

_____

Learning to meditate, discovering the energy around you, and dwelling on your feelings, together form a model for you to develop your psychic skills. Learning about yourself and discovering how you react gives you a high level of control when you are in situations that require you to be in a sensitive state. Clairsentience is usually the first psychic sense that we notice. The next Psychic Minute defines psychic touch, also known as clairtangency or psychometry. It can be a mechanism to access any of your abilities but most commonly a "door opener" to clairsentience.

Psychic Minute Fifteen

Psychic touch, also known as clairtangency or psychometry, is the soul's capacity to use a physical experience to capture information "beyond the physical" from people, objects, and/ or animals.

The ability to use your sense of touch to capture information is very interesting because we use this quality without realizing it. A handshake, hug, kiss, or other physical contact affects us in many ways. Physical contact, however, does not just involve your skin touching another person. Sounds, pictures, smells, and other physical sensations touch us and affect us emotionally and psychically. Touching affects us positively and negatively depending upon the person or situation. Once this concept is understood, you will learn that most psychic experiences can be derived from a psychic touch experience.

Soul Exercise

Cut out pictures (or have someone else do it) from a magazine and put them in blank envelopes. Mix them up. Focus on one of the envelopes and record what comes to you. Write down the impression that you receive from the imprinted energy within the envelope. For example, you may notice male or female energy. You may notice feelings such as sadness or happiness. You may notice visual impression such as colors or other energies that may give you clues about the pictures. Record you observations here. _____

These impressions that you receive help you develop confidence in yourself.

Psychic Minute Sixteen

Clairvoyance, or "clear vision", is the voluntary and/or involuntary ability of the human soul to access visual information solely within the mind, and it can happen suddenly and without warning.

This fascinating psychic sense has many variables, and there are several different ways to experience it. It has at least seven variations that the mind uses to provide us with information. These include:

1. Pictures, symbols, and fragments
2. Seeing past, current or future events (premonitions, déjà vu, prophecies, etc.)
3. Auras
4. Remote viewing
5. Dreams (color or black and white)
6. Astral projection
7. Observing spirits

Each of these variations deserves special attention. They are all unique, but they are all visual experiences.

Soul Exercise

What memorable images have you received about a person or event that proved to be very accurate?

_____

_____

Clairvoyance is fascinating because a picture <u>is</u> worth a thousand words, and it is satisfying to see the unknown. Many people say, "Seeing is believing." The validation of a visual image removes ambiguity and gives the viewer a certainty of fact. Skepticism has no boundaries, and even a picture can be misinterpreted. Clairvoyance, however, can often be validated with other psychic senses, such as hearing. We might believe something that we hear, for example, even when we do not believe what we see.

Psychic Minute Seventeen

Clairaudience is the soul's capacity to capture audio information beyond the physical limits of the ears.

The study and development of psychic senses ranges from very easy to difficult. Thus far, we have discussed clairsentience, clairtangency, and clairvoyance. They are more commonly identified because most people can relate to an experience with each of them. This is not the case with clairaudience, clairgustance, clairfragrance, or claircognizance. These senses may take more time to notice and refine as you progress with your journey to develop your psychic abilities.

The clairaudient individual may say that they do not have the same emotional or visual experiences of those with strong clairsentient or clairvoyant abilities. Their experiences are auditory, and they pay attention to an inner voice communicating with them. This sense is a healthy quality; however, the disease of schizophrenia can be confused with this psychic sense.

Hearing a *clear voice* is a matter of paying attention and trusting the information received. Tapping into clairaudience involves using your usual techniques. Meditating, identifying your personal hearing space, paying attention to words you hear, and practice are essential elements in developing your clairaudience.

Psychic Minute Eighteen

Clairgustance is the recognition of a particular taste sensation in your mouth without any explanation of the origin.

As with the other senses, it can occur suddenly and for no apparent reason. Again, like the other senses, psychic tastes may be captured consciously, subconsciously or involuntarily. Many people are able to capture these tastes, but they do not recognize them as metaphysical senses. It is not until they review different circumstances in their lives that they are able to make the association.

Psychic Minute Nineteen

Clairfragrance is the human quality to capture scents beyond the physical limitations of the olfactory glands.

Your nose can detect scents on a psychic level, and it can also notice smells directly associated with spirits.

Soul Exercise

Can you relate to a moving clairaudient, clairgustant, or clairfragrant experience?

_____

_____

We will now shift our attention away from features of the body such as the eyes and ears to the mind, and therefore shift our perspective.

Psychic Minute Twenty

Intuition, claircognizance, is the soul's capacity to receive 'ideas' from beyond the limitations of the mind.

Intuition is often confused with the other psychic senses and is used in a generic sense. However, the principal ability involves the mind and your thinking. The other senses allow your intuition to be stimulated, but it is a thought 'dropping into your mind' that allows you to have a 'knowing' about a person, event, or situation.

Practicing how intuition works with you can be accomplished with puzzle exercises, video games, or playing charades. Playing card games involves skill, but a little intuition can be the edge you need to be successful. Paying attention, observing behavior, and trusting information are all keys to understanding the way intuition works in your life.

Soul Exercise

What situations can you identify using your intuition?

_____

_____

The use of intuition is another powerful tool for you to use as you develop your psychic skills. It is part of "putting it all together" and understanding these abilities. Looking at your psychic profile is just the beginning of your Psychic Journey.

Learning to use your abilities will "stretch" you and cause you to be more aware of your surroundings. Observing with your physical senses is very natural, and when you start observing with your psychic extended senses, you will notice the world is very different place. Your perspective changes and your attitudes towards situations and people will be modified or validated to a higher degree.

Soul Meditation #3

In this meditation you will need to focus on a particular question and allow your psychic senses to seek information about it. Allow your soul's energy to find psychic impressions to help you determine the answers.

Chapter Review

Describe the following psychic senses:

Clairsentience _____

Clairvoyance _____

Clairaudience _____

Clairgustance _____

Clairfragrance _____

Claircognizance_____

CHAPTER FOUR

PSYCHIC FEELING

She said, "I just felt something was going to happen," so she decided not to drive to the store that day. It was a good thing since there was a major accident that occurred at just the time she was scheduled to go. Some called it luck, others coincidence, but she knew it was more than that. She understood her feelings and acted upon them.

When we think of energy, we usually think of electricity or another form of power that turns something on or makes something move. However, when it comes to your psychic abilities, it is not this type of energy that activates them. Your soul or psychic senses receive information from people, places, animals, objects, and sounds. When energy is accepted by your personal space, it can be immediately interpreted, and your response is usually emotional.

This immediate interpretation can be defined as a psychic feeling, or *clairsentience*. In this chapter, we take a closer look at clairsentience. It is considered the first psychic sense because most people use it more than any other. Our easily accessible emotions are part of our humanness. They make us unique.

Psychic Minute Twenty-One

Clairsentience is the soul's ability to consciously and/or unconsciously capture 'feeling' or emotional information beyond the limitations of your physical nervous system.

Feelings are often captured on an involuntarily basis and known on a subconscious level as well. We are able to understand and study our emotions through experiences. We notice our psychic feelings (emotions) in common situations such as first impressions, hunches, and gut feelings. They can come to us suddenly and without warning.

Soul Exercise

Recall emotional responses you had during happy, sad and neutral occasions to assist you with developing your clairsentience.

Here are some examples of happy occasions:

1. A birthday party
2. The birth of a child
3. A graduation
4. A wedding
5. A New Year's Eve party

Here are some examples of sad occasions:

1. The loss of a game by a favorite team
2. A funeral
3. The loss of a job
4. A divorce
5. Reading about a violent crime

Soul Exercise

A *first impression* is an emotional response and energy imprint you receive when you first meet a person or learn about a situation. The emotional imprint you receive is beyond the physical and is usually correct. A common situation where you might form a first impression is when meeting the new boyfriend or girlfriend of a loved one. Your psychic emotions may be in conflict with your expectations. You may defer to those you care about because you want them to be happy, and you may not want to express a negative opinion. First impressions can work in the positive just as well as the negative. Sometimes seeing a person or experiencing a situation that may appear to be negative with your physical senses can turn out to be a positive.

Recall one of your first impressions about a person that you dismissed but later learned was correct.

_____

_____

Psychic feelings can also be used when solving problems. This form of the sense is called a *hunch*. For example, when investigating a problematic situation where evidence is not clear, a psychic feeling may be the leap that is needed to "connect the dots" or make sense of data. A third form of psychic feeling is commonly referred to as a *gut feeling*. This type of emotion is a premonition of a future event.

Psychic feelings can be acquired when you walk into a room. You can sense energy in an empty room from previous conversations or actions. For example, an act of violence leaves an impression that can be sensed by your emotions. By the same token, you can sense energy from people in a room as soon as you walk into it. The information can be detailed in either case. However, most often, you may ignore this energy because it is contrary to your logic, and you dismiss these *sudden*, unexplained feelings. The conflict occurs when your physical senses are telling you one thing, and your emotions are telling you something different. It is like going into a fun house at a carnival where things are not actually as they appear.

Unexplained feelings are not taken seriously because there is no logic associated with them. Impressions may not make sense until a situation unfolds, and the fleeting information is validated. At that point, you find yourself questioning why you did not accept your initial feelings. Initial acceptance often can save you time, effort, and aggravation since psychic feelings just arrive without trying or having to provoke them.

Psychic Minute Twenty-Two

Sudden feelings are usually associated with imminent danger or immediate action.

Having a feeling before a storm or an impending accident are two examples of sudden feelings. They are not always associated with a person or a known situation like a first impression. In addition, they are more immediate than a gut feeling because there is no problem or original concept involved. Sudden emotions often indicate a defensive action is needed. They assist you in being on guard and help raise your adrenaline.

When you have sudden feelings, the personal space around you is activated. In some cases, your entire body can be affected with a feeling, and recognizing it can be difficult without some practice. When you are not practiced, you may only recognize the importance of the feeling after it is too late to use it to change or explain an outcome.

Soul Exercise

Name a typical emotional experience you could not explain but later made sense.

_____

_____

Clairsentience, as a psychic ability and a part of your soul's energy, stretches you and increases your "perspective" of life. Observing and paying attention to your emotions takes time. Meditation can be used as a tool to focus on your emotions. Dwelling on them is essential if you are going to recognize them in your everyday life. It gives you clues about the way we receive emotional data outside of the safe environment of meditation. Meditation is a method used to practice pushing out your personal space and expanding your field of sensitivity. Pushing out your personal space is like having a net of energy attempting to capture other energy.

Imagine sitting in an eggshell of white light, and it is close to the skin. This white light around the body is the energy of the soul. In the case of clairsentience, it is the area on the body called the solar plexus. We have the ability to enlarge this field around us like a net, noticing the solar plexus area, and it can receive energy emitted by another person. At first, this net may appear to be very porous, but with practice, the net can be tightened. Practice allows you to sense and interpret information quickly and accurately. We have a natural ability to capture information, but it can be enhanced by exercising the soul in this manner. Once you are confident about the energy you are sensing, you can judge a situation through your feelings. Learning to trust and discern is the most difficult part of learning about clairsentience.

Psychic Minute Twenty-Three

Empathy is a physical response sensing the emotions of another person.

Each person's soul has a natural frequency and range that can be developed. Some people can develop it more than others, but everyone has the ability to some degree. Our feelings are some of the most important aspects of life, and without feelings, one does not have compassion or empathy. This is not normal and can be problematic. At the other extreme are *empaths*. They are people who are extremely sensitive to the energy of others. There must be a balance.

Most people who say they do not have feelings are simply not paying attention. Some people do not give themselves permission to acknowledge their feelings, and they hide them. The idea of giving yourself "permission" to have feelings is essential in developing your psychic skills.

For example, society gives women permission to cry. However, men are not given this opportunity as readily and are expected to control and not express their feelings. It is perceived as a sign of strength, and a man who is seen crying is often described as weak or unstable. This stereotypical standard does not reflect the reality that women and men both have strong emotions and need healthy outlets for them. Crying is a healthy outlet.

Soul Exercise

Recount a moment when you experienced these emotions?

Happiness? _____

Sadness? _____

Indifference? _____

Anger? _____

Others? _____

Psychic Minute Twenty-Four

Sympathy pains are actual pains we may experience when we are aware of another person's health condition.

Sympathy pains that are psychic occur when you receive a pain and know it relates to another person without any prior knowledge.

Society sends mixed signals about feelings. Generally speaking, it does not accept the practice of our psychic feelings, but it does not want us to be in denial, either. This confusing message must be sorted out on an individual basis. It is important to learn about yourself as an individual and not buy into all of society's constraints. Developing your own opinions and self-esteem assists you in defining a self-image. We have to understand how we feel about ourselves, our world, etc. before we can move forward. Many times, we must give ourselves permission to have feelings.

We learn to explore our feelings, recognizing and controlling them immediately. We use our souls as a source of understanding, for it is our souls that capture the emotional energy initially. Our psychic feelings can then be used effectively with practice.

Soul Exercise

A journal with the details of your clairsentient experiences can be helpful as you develop and understand your psychic abilities. A journal reflects an individual's personality and assists in developing a psychic profile. We are all different, and there are no good or bad approaches to looking for answers. There is no right or wrong way to keep records or to keep a journal. Once you understand the impressions or images that come to you, you can begin to better understand yourself and others.

Use your journal to record experiences of an emotional nature using expressions such as "I felt." Your journal will assist you in identifying new experiences involving your emotions. You need to note the differences between the emotions you feel from being provoked and those you experience that are not provoked.

After you post your events in a journal, it is important to study the information. If the events can be understood and perhaps memorized, the process of sorting them out will become clearer. The insights gained will be beneficial and will build confidence.

Soul Exercise

Do you have sudden feelings about people or situations without any provocation?

_____

_____

Do you often feel drained or nauseous or have headaches or other physical sensations after being in a crowd?

_____

_____

Do you have emotional first impressions about individuals or situations?

_____

_____

Do you find you are often alone because you have to recharge your energy?

_____

_____

Do you often say, "I just felt I knew the answer?"

_____

_____

Do your emotions allow you to have visions, hear solutions to issues, or just know answers to problems?

_____

_____

Soul Meditation #4 – Clairsentience

This meditation is about tuning into your feelings and learning to measure them for future reference. You will want to simulate emotions in a safe environment so that when they strike you in your everyday life, you will recognize them immediately. You must stretch your emotions and identify them when they are encountered. There may not be time to evaluate an emotion when it comes to you unexpectedly, so knowing them before they are captured or sensed by your soul's energy is very important.

Once you have settled down and relaxed, you can begin using your imagination to simulate your emotions. Imagine being with a newborn baby boy. Notice how you feel being around this new life that is totally helpless. This individual offers promise for the future but is unable to take care of any of his own needs. You feel the male energy around this child and the positive aspects of being near a new life. Dwell on this energy for a moment. Sense the joy and happiness.

After you have been here for a while, begin to shift your attention. Move forward and imagine the energy of a five year old little boy. This child is able to move around and is able to communicate his needs to you but remains very dependent upon others. This little boy is interested in toys like cars, army men, kites, and Legos. He is happy, and the energy surrounding him makes you feel positive. You know this child is not yet ready to be on his own, and yet he is very different from the newborn baby you were near just a few moments ago. Dwell on this energy for a few moments before you move on to the next scenario.

Begin to shift your attention, and notice that you are around a thirteen-year-old boy. He can ride a bike and use a mobile phone. This young man may be athletic and be an expert at video games. He is growing quickly, and you feel the energy around him. You notice his strength and his growing independence. He is not yet ready to be on his own, but soon he will be grown. Dwell on this energy and notice the way you feel around this young person.

Once you have been here for a few moments, it is time to shift again. Notice that you are around a young man who has just graduated from college. This young man is full of hope and ambition. He is ready to be an independent adult and start making his mark on the world. You feel happy and proud for this young person who has accomplished so much in his few years. Dwell on this energy, and notice all of the emotions you are experiencing at this time. Stay here for a few more moments before you move on and experience new emotions.

Shift your attention again and begin to notice this young man is now around thirty years old. He is a father and a husband. He has responsibilities and is an active member of the community. This man is fully independent, and you have experienced his growth from infancy to adulthood. Dwell here for a few moments and notice how you feel around him.

Once you have spent some time with your feelings towards this young man as an independent adult, you can begin to shift your attention again. Notice this young man in a police officer's uniform. How do you feel when you are around a police officer? You notice that you feel respect and honor him as a person who has devoted his life to law enforcement. These feelings of respect are in addition to the feelings you have experienced knowing him as a young man, father, and husband. They are definable for you, and when you feel them around someone in your everyday experiences, you will remember them. Dwell on these feelings for a moment. Explore them until you have become comfortable with them.

Now that you have become familiar with these feelings, you will need to shift again. Shift back to knowing this young man just as a husband and father. These are becoming base feelings for you. Once you are back to a familiar point, you will need to shift again. This time, shift your attention to this young man and notice him as a doctor.

Feel the respect you have for this man as a doctor. Notice the trust you have in him for his education and his knowledge in the medical field. The accomplishment of becoming a doctor is significant, and you innately recognize the position he has achieved. He is a person that you may need to depend on for your greatest health need, and you feel the magnitude of having someone like him around you.

Once you have dwelled on these feelings, begin to shift again. This is when you shift back to your original feelings of this young man as an adult who is a husband and father. Notice the changes within you as you go through this exercise. Once you are at this point, begin to let go all of your feelings toward him and clear yourself of all emotions. Stay here for a few moments and just enjoy the feeling of nothingness around you.

After you have been here for a while, you begin to visualize the presence of a baby girl. This baby girl is precious beyond belief, and you notice your feelings around her. She is helpless and must have her every need met by others. Her mother may be near her assisting her with everything to make her comfortable and happy. You notice you have a sense of joy and happiness around her.

You feel a sense of being protective and vigilant toward her. Your senses are heightened, and you know that you are will care for her. You stay here a moment and dwell on all of the feelings you have around this newborn child who offers so much hope and goodness for the future. Your thoughts and feelings are very tender and precious at this time.

You begin to shift your attention and imagine this little girl at the age of five. She is far more independent than she was the time you first saw her. She is verbal and is able to do many things for herself, but she remains dependent upon the adults around her. It is necessary for her parents to be there and assist her with her many needs. Notice how you feel about this little girl who is playing with dolls and has a special twinkle in her eye. She captures your heart, and you feel a strong loving bond with her as your feelings toward her continue to be very positive and hopeful.

Stay here a few moments and dwell on the happiness of being around this very young person who brings you joy from just being around her. You begin to shift your attention again and move forward in her life. You find that you are now around a young lady in her early teens. This young woman is very independent, may have her own telephone, and can ride a bike. She has friends and is involved in many activities. How does this energy feel around this young person who is vibrant with life and demonstrating so much promise for the future?

Notice that you are able to have a conversation with her, and notice the feeling of amazement about her intelligence and knowledge of the world. You continue to realize that she is not yet ready to take on the world on her own, but she is being prepared to be a strong, independent adult. She will soon be driving a car and gaining responsibility. You feel proud and recognize the changes that you have undergone since you first saw her as an infant. Stay here a few moments and dwell on your feelings at this time and notice the energy around you and this young girl.

Begin to shift your energy again and see her as a young woman who has just graduated from college. She is beaming with joy and confidence over her accomplishment of finishing school. She is full of determination to make her way in the world, and you feel that sense of accomplishment with her. Notice your feelings of love and respect for her and see that she is now the independent adult that she needs to be in order to face the challenges of the world.

Stay here a few moments as you dwell on this time in this young woman's life and feel the energy surrounding the joy of it. Remain here until you are ready to move on to the next scene. Once you are ready, you can begin to shift your attention again. This time, you see her as a wife and mother.

Notice the way you feel about her. She is an adult who is a responsible member of the community, and she is handling those new duties very well. You have been there since the beginning and have travelled with her through her journey in life. It has been a growth experience for both of you, and you feel joy and happiness for her for reaching this point. Dwell on this time for a few moments, and sense your feelings throughout the process.

Once you have been here a while, you can begin to shift your attention again. This time, you see this young woman as a police officer. Notice the changes in your feelings around her. She is not just a responsible wife and mother, she is a person who commands your respect for the position she holds. You feel the importance of the work she does upholding the laws of the community. Stay here a while and dwell on your feelings. Notice the way your attitude and disposition have changed to match the current situation.

After you have stayed here for a few moments, you shift back to your feelings towards this young woman as a wife and mother. Once you are back to this point, stay here for a moment. Begin to shift your attention again and notice this young lady as a doctor. Observe the way you feel about her as a person in the medical profession. You feel a respect and trust that you have never felt before around her because of her status as a physician.

Just as you felt the weight of this position for the young man that you previously had dwelled upon, you now notice the same level of respect for her that you had for him. She is also a person you may call on to be there in your time of need. Her knowledge and skill may be needed to save you from a serious situation, and this thought alone creates certain feelings about this young woman.

Now that you have been dwelling on this situation, the way you feel about the young woman begins to shift again. You go back to your feelings about her as a wife and mother. Stay here again, and you begin to let go of all feelings. Begin to reflect on the shifts you have just experienced during this exercise.

You have stretched your feelings to different levels, and these feelings matched the situation that you imagined at the time. You do this naturally in your everyday life, and it is done with your psychic sense of clairsentience as well. You may not notice it as much with your extended feelings, but it happens to you on a regular basis. Now that you have completed this exercise, it is up to you to notice your feelings change when situations change quickly or unexpectedly in your life.

Unexpected feelings must be quickly recognized and evaluated by your physical senses and your logical mind. You will be able to act appropriately to future situations because you are practiced in responding to your psychic abilities even though they may appear irrational. You learn to trust the unusual because you know it is your soul that has captured the energy to make your emotions signal you about change.

A careful psychic recognizes emotional energy and acts with an appropriate and controlled response. Reacting to a chaotic situation by recognizing and respecting it can result in a positive outcome. It is the rational psychic who can do this with great skill and a cool resolve.

Chapter Review

1. Give a definition of clairsentience.
2. What is a first impression?
3. What is an example of a "sudden feeling"?
4. How does clairsentience affect your life?
5. Practice meditating on past psychic feelings.

CHAPTER FIVE

PSYCHIC TOUCH

INTRODUCTION

Psychic feelings are nuanced by psychic touch. The physical sensation of touch allows you to interpret emotions around a subject. For example, if someone wants the energy of a ring to be interpreted, information such as previous ownership, origin of the ring, and events surrounding it can be analyzed simply through touch. It can also provide insight about the circumstances under which the person acquired the ring. If the ring has had multiple owners, it can reveal information about previous owners and whether they are alive or in spirit. Energy from the ring or the psychic touch subject can also serve as "door openers" for other psychic abilities to be activated. It can even allow spirits to contact you. This chapter is divided into four sections: 1) Psychic Touch Definition, 2) Psychic Imprinting, 3) Receiving Energy, and 4) Understanding the Energy.

DEFINITION

The development of your psychic abilities is a journey of self-discovery, and learning about your psychic touch is part of this journey. As a refresher from earlier in this workbook, psychic touch, also known as psychometry or clairtangency, is defined as *the soul's capacity to use a physical experience to capture information "beyond the physical" from people, objects, and/or animals.*

The ability to use your sense of touch to capture information is very interesting because we use this quality without realizing it. The soul's energy is part of the sensitivity of your skin. This is why it is able to acquire energy from people, objects, or other physical experiences. A handshake, hug, kiss, or other physical contact affects us in many ways. Physical contact, however, does not just involve our skin touching another person. Sounds, pictures, smells, and other physical sensations "touch" us and affect us emotionally and psychically. Touching affects us positively and negatively depending upon the person or circumstances. Once this concept is understood, we learn that most psychic experiences can be derived from a psychic touch moment.

The difference between a psychic touch experience and other psychic experiences is the *physical aspect* of the event. Other psychic events do not have a physical experience catalyst to create them. They are spontaneous and come from beyond the physical on their own. Psychic touch has a stimulus that induces our psychic senses to start operating.

Our focus with this portion of this chapter is on the physical touch of the skin and the voice. Holding an object, touching a person or thing, or hearing a voice or sound gives us a heightened sense of our psychic abilities. The experience of a physical "touch" is a powerful affirmation of energy. Experience with different sensations allows a person to understand them and, as a result, "read" them with great accuracy.

Soul Exercise

Have you ever had an experience with psychic touch?"

_____

_____

We have identified a definition of psychic touch and have discussed a perspective on common experiences. Focusing on personal experiences and the impressions left by them will assist you in working with your abilities and becoming more confident using them. This awareness brings us to our next Psychic Minute and a discussion of energy.

PSYCHIC IMPRINTING

Psychic Minute Twenty-Five

Humans are physical and spiritual beings who emit and receive energy.
Imprinted energy emits a low but intense frequency that can be detected and followed with psychic senses. The energy we emit can be left behind when we no longer hold an object or when we are no longer in a place. Once an item is touched, a connection is made by the person who does the touching.

The energy we place on people, places, and things can still be sensed at a later time. Good feelings, for example, can be felt by others after we are no longer present since there is a residual effect left by our energy. A crime scene, for example, leaves the trauma of the moment at the scene. Imprints come from the strangest things, and it is difficult to know which object will hold the strongest imprint until the energy emission is actually felt. Practice, practice, practice, is the best way to begin to understand and to capture energy from imprints.

Soul Exercise

Can you give examples of detecting energy from a place after a person has left or after a situation has taken place?

_____

_____

You are constantly receiving messages from the people, places, pets, and objects that you encounter. You simply may not realize that the messages are imprints. In your everyday life, you imprint a bit of your personality and experiences on the people and things you touch. And, by the same token, you are imprinted by other people and events in your life. This fact may be very obvious to you once it is brought to your attention, but what is not so obvious is the fact that these unseen imprints can be read by people.

Psychic Minute Twenty-Six

An energy imprint is a residual impression of life experiences from a person which is left on another person, place, object, or living thing (i.e. an animal).

Humans are physical and spiritual beings who emit and receive energy. Imprinted energy emits a low but intense frequency that can be detected and followed with psychic senses. The energy we emit can be left behind when we no longer hold an object or when we are no longer in a place. Once an item is touched, a connection is made by the person who does the touching.

The energy we place on people, places, and things can still be sensed at a later time. Good feelings, for example, can be felt by others after we are no longer present since there is a residual effect left by our energy. In contrast, a crime scene leaves the trauma of the moment at the scene. Imprints come from the strangest things, and it is difficult to know which object will hold the strongest imprint until the energy emission is actually felt. Practice, practice, practice, is the best way to begin to understand and to capture energy from imprints.

Capturing energy is a matter of identifying information "striking" your soul. We sense an energy field and distinguish the emotions related to it. If you have ever walked into a room and sensed that there was an argument going on, you have picked up the force of the emotions left from the people who had the argument. Your soul is familiar with human energy and can interpret it. During the course of your life, your soul learns and gains experience from your everyday routine.

The concept of a "life experience" involves any and every experience you have ever had. This includes your happy and sad moments. Life experiences are not just "moments in time" or fleeting events. They are periods in your life that can be life-long or very short. Relationships that imprint may include: marriage, divorce, relationships with friends, children, and co-workers. They may include events that are happy, sad, tragic, or violent. The intensity of the emotional experience determines the degree of imprint left and the degree of its importance.

Energy imprints are everywhere, but it is the intensity of the imprint that is important. A chair in a classroom, the seat on a mass transit vehicle, the knives and forks at restaurants, used clothing, jewelry, pictures, and family pets are common sources of energy imprints. Most of these examples carry imprints from several people. The longer a person is around a place, object, pet, or other person, the greater the intensity of the imprint.

An energy imprint works like a magnet that has touched a piece of metal leaving tiny particles on this other metal. The receiving metal accepts the particles and gives a sense that it is magnetized. This lasts as long as the magnetized particles remain on the metal. This is similar to the way we leave energy imprints on people and things we touch. Imprints are left all over our homes. Our furniture is like a magnet accepting our energy and the energy of everyone else who comes in contact with it. Over a period of years, the power of this imprinted energy can influence the feeling of the room.

Sometimes our rooms feel heavy, and we feel the need to redecorate. When furniture in a room is changed, the energy in it is freshened and the feeling is lightened. Since the imprints of the furniture have been removed, the same room now has different energy. A fresh coat of paint can have a similar effect.

There may be no better place to practice gathering imprint feelings than in an antique store. Energies from the old objects are all over the place. It will be obvious to even a beginning practitioner that some antiques will have high energy imprints while others have little or none. A beautiful piece of furniture, ceramic, or other item can be deflated by a grumpy original owner. A not-so-pretty piece can exude the happiness of a home that appreciated it. When choosing an antique, pay attention to what is going on inside. How does the antique make you feel? Touch it, if possible, and see what response there is to the touch. Sensing energy from an object sets the tone for your relationship with it, and this can be the difference between loving and hating the object.

We can sense good or compatible energy around us in cars, houses, places of business, indoors or even outside. We can also sense danger, negative energies, and even unhealthy places or objects. Jewelry from another person may be rejected by some people because they find the energy of the previous owner to be incompatible with theirs. This may be a psychological reaction, or it may be a psychic response. There are other people who want to wear another person's jewelry in order to experience the energy from the original owner.

Antique stores may be filled with both good and not-so-good energy. If you attempt to interpret details from the object's imprint, the information cannot be verified as a rule, since you generally do not know about the previous owner. Information received may be fragmented, or vague, or you may be trying too hard. Linking the information may be difficult. Sometimes, you know that the energy draws you in, but you do not know why. Be able to distinguish whether this strong pull is positive or negative. Also, there may be times when an object may not give off any recognizable energy information at all until later. Having a delayed reaction to an object is part of personal development and should be recognized as such. Beware of the impulse to buy everything that "feels" like it speaks to you.

When an object has been touched by many people, you will still sense energies on the objects, but it is difficult to interpret what specific energies contributed since there are multiple impressions with less intensity. A piece of jewelry or an object with one owner is more easily definable. The energy is pure and intense. Life experiences from the owner can be defined and sensed from the object since a person's life experiences are left with it. You are able to sense the imprinter's experiences by seeing, feeling, and knowing them with your psychic abilities. Generally, the first impression when picking up an object is the sense of whether the owner was male or female. Once this connection is made, the energy may help determine the relationship between the previous and current owners. It will indicate if the previous owner was a child, relative, friend, grandparent, or some other person. Familiar energy often indicates a relative. The feeling of whether or not the person is alive is discernible by an experienced psychic. A practiced individual can distinguish these differences because they draw from their inventory of feelings and memories to detect the type of energy coming from the object.

Soul Exercise

Dwell on the following types of energy:

What does it feel like to touch an object belonging to a man?
- Bring these feelings out further and dwell on the energy of feelings for a father, husband, brother, son, male child, grandfather and an uncle.
- Bring these feelings further and associate other emotions with each of them such as happiness, sadness, anger or violence.

What does it feel like to touch an object belonging to a woman?
- Bring these feelings out further and dwell on the energy of feelings for a mother, wife, sister, daughter, female child, grandmother and an aunt.
- Bring these feelings further and associate other emotions with each of them such as happiness, sadness, anger or violence.

What does it feel like to touch an object associated with an animal?
- Use your imagination to dwell on a particular animal such as a dog, cat, horse or another pet you may have or had in the past.

In our everyday lives, we imprint a bit of our personalities and experiences on the people and the things that we influence. By the same token, we are imprinted by other people and by other objects we encounter.

When you are attempting to interpret feelings that you receive from a picture or object, you can be confused until the owner of the object or an informed person verifies some of the information that you have discerned. Once you receive clarification, with experience, you can sense other energy with a high degree of accuracy without verification. It is as if the information was stored in a crumpled ball, and we could only read the pieces around the edges. Once you get a bit of clarity, the ball unfolds, and a much greater amount of information becomes apparent.

Understanding and interpreting this imprinted energy comes from your memories and feelings during your past personal experiences. Previous experiences can give you clues about what you can expect from a situation, and you already have a picture in your mind about how something makes you "feel". You can anticipate smells, tastes, pictures, and feelings because of these past impressions.

Another instance of imprinted energy we sense is not with pictures or impression, but with associations. The energies between couples are easily discernible. Partners can read their partner's energy. They can know their thoughts and anticipate their actions. Two people in a long relationship can even look at each other and finish a sentence or know what to do without a word being spoken. Sometimes, they can even begin to resemble each other.

Distant imprints can be so strong that partners or even friends can sense what is happening. A strong emotion can be felt even though the two people may be miles apart. Instances of such mental contact can be recounted by spouses and partners, by children and parents, by siblings, and other closely associated people.

Imprinted energies are best identified by seeing, feeling, and knowing through your psychic abilities. Psychic touch is a powerful tool and can be used in ordinary life. It can be used during a job interview or just when you want to learn about another person. You can exercise your psychic energy and read imprints by holding something a person has touched. The process of testing your ability to read imprinted energies can be rewarding.

Energy imprints do not have a life span or period when they are no longer readable. They are permanent unless they are removed. The most common way to remove the energy is to change the object by destruction. This can be done by changing the molecular structure of the object through melting or burning it. It should be noted that the use of sage, sound vibrations, or other means to clear energy are also forms of destroying or altering an imprint. Even then, the energy may still remain as a residual imprint of the person who left it behind.

A good example of this type of energy is a photograph. They say that a picture is "worth a thousand words", and this expression is true for our purposes. Native Americans have said that a picture takes part of one's soul when it is taken. The residual energy from it can often give you impressions of events surrounding people and their feelings at the time the photo was taken. Furthermore, you do not need to see the picture to obtain sensations from it. A practiced person can receive information from a picture by holding it in the dark or in an envelope.

The energy we emit lets people know who we are, and the energy we receive tells us about others. For example, we can tell if a person is happy or sad, if they are sick or recovering from an illness, if they have a relationship issue or financial problems, or if they have issues with a co-worker. People emit specific stresses, and you can feel them with great accuracy without them communicating this to you. Sensing this type of information is often astonishing to those who are projecting it. As we extend energy, and as we receive energy, we may capture either bits and pieces or large amounts of information. It depends upon how the energy strikes our personal space. As psychics, we must pay attention to the information we receive and interpret it carefully. While we may learn some things about others, we do not know everything. We must be careful not to pass judgment using our personal mores. For instance, if you are feeling that another person is unemployed for an extended period of time, you cannot infer that the person is lazy. You only know that they are unemployed. Clairsentience and psychic ability often do not portray everything about a person's personality or circumstances. When giving private consultations, you should not violate confidences.

Soul Exercise

Have you ever received information from a picture (without looking at it) that gave you accurate psychic information?

_____

_____

We have been discussing energy imprinting and have been concentrating on imprints created by touch or on a picture. Our next Psychic Minute is about imprinting by sound. A sound imprint or a voice imprint can impact a person's psyche and last a lifetime. This is true with a positive or a negative sound.

Psychic Minute Twenty-Seven

A sound imprint is an energy imprint created by a person, animal, or event revealing reality beyond the physical limits of our human hearing.

The voice of a person is a pathway to a person's life and experiences. We often detect emotions in the voices of people when they are in distress. However, we can also detect information about people even when they do not physically appear to have stress around them. The energy of the vocal sound is detected when it enters your personal space, and it can then be interpreted. Divorce, grief, job loss, ill health, and other experiences can be sensed from speech. A person's voiceprint reveals much about the events in his or her life. Voice mapping is a new scientific approach analyzing this energy.

A lie detector test measures the responses to questions, and these responses by the body are often heightened once a verbal remark is made. The voice reveals stresses created by an untruth while a true answer allows a person to remain calm. Experience hearing voices will allow you to detect stresses and discern their meanings with accuracy. You may often hear someone say, "I heard the sadness in their voice," or another similar expression.

When a person says his/her name, the sound touches your personal space, and the vocal sound opens energy pathways. These pathways can be followed by your psychic senses with amazing accuracy.

We have identified a definition of psychic touch and have indicated a perspective on common experiences. Focusing on personal experiences and impressions received will assist you in working with your abilities and becoming more confident using them.

Soul Exercise

What experience can you recall in which you received an impression from a sound that gave you accurate Psychic information?

_____

_____

Psychic Minute Twenty-Eight

Psychic information is most valuable when it can be independently verified.

Verifiable information and the sense of knowing how this information came to you is a good indicator of the validity of non-verifiable information. Once it becomes validated, you have achieved a high level of accuracy through verification, and you will develop confidence and be able to use your talents with assurance. The ability to understand your psychic feelings exercises and stretches your soul.

Information should be used only with discretion and without judgment. The information you receive is just energy and has no moral agenda. Your logical mind creates an opinion from the information that you receive.

RECEIVING ENERGY

Psychic Minute Twenty-Nine

Imprinted energy emits a low frequency we can detect and follow with our psychic senses.

Once you touch something, you should immediately make a connection with the item you are touching. This connection will be made with one or all of your psychic senses. The soul uses the impressions and interprets them with different psychic senses. It could appear in your mind with your sight, hearing, smell, or taste. It may also appear with a feeling, and the feeling should be recognizable.

The low energy output from the imprinted energy will enter your personal space via your skin, the receptor for the energy. The imprint is filled with information you can interpret if you pay attention to it. This energy has paths or "strings" to follow, and one person may notice a path that another person will not notice. It is an individual opportunity for everyone, and unless the imprinted energy on the object has been "removed" (as discussed earlier in this chapter), it is permanent.

Generally, the first impression about the energy will be whether it is male or female. Once this connection is made, you will be able to "push" the energy and use your psychic senses to determine if the energy is that of a child, brother, sister, friend, husband, wife, mother, father, grandparent or other person. Each of them has energy around them, and it will be familiar because you know the feeling you have when you are around people in your life fitting these descriptions.

The feeling of whether or not the person is alive or deceased is also discernable. You will notice that you are developing a profile for the object's energy. A sort of "map" is generated, and you will be following it. Discovering new information about a living person or making a connection with a spirit is now possible. You have now made a leap from the low energy of the imprint to a higher energy.

It is more comfortable to work with this higher energy than low energy, and it is easier to maneuver with it. The information comes in a stream and is not just residual. You no longer have to dwell on the energy received to understand it because it is current and relevant.

The ability to use psychic touch is a very powerful tool and can be used in your everyday life. This skill is useful, for example, in job interviews or just to learn about another person. Holding something that someone else has touched is very revealing. Write down impressions as they come to help you with your "energy mapping" and use your rational mind to interpret information.

Soul Exercise

Have you ever held an object and had a sudden feeling about it?

_____

_____

UNDERSTANDING THE ENERGY

Psychic Minute Thirty

Psychic touch, or psychometry, requires a clear mind and the self-knowledge concerning your ability to capture energy.

Preparing to do psychic touch is easy, but it requires patience and practice. It requires a clear mind and knowledge of your personal sensitivity. You need to be able to recognize energy and read the energy with known samples. Learning to focus and pay attention are also essential for psychic work as you have to accept the energy and not judge it; just state the nature of the energy received. Finally, dwelling on this energy allows you to recognize and understand it when you are not expecting it.

You need to understand your needs when you are trying to use your psychic touch. It is an individual decision whether or not to use devices when clearing and preparing for psychometry. Some people drink water or use essential oils to enhance sensitivity. Meditation before reading an object is a good ritual for anyone, but practice should help you avoid requiring these types of preparation tools.

Soul Exercise

Has information you received from psychic touch ever been verified?

_____

_____

We use our Psychic abilities interchangeably with our physical senses. We may be unaware we are doing it, but it is one of the things that makes us uniquely human. We are blessed to be spiritual beings and have so many talents and abilities. It is normal to discount our psychic abilities because they are not as accepted as our physical abilities.

Once you learn to pay attention to energies around you, you can be more fully human. Accepting that you have the ability to sense existence beyond the physical allows you to learn about yourself and helps you grow personally.

Chapter Review

1. Give a definition of psychic touch.
2. Describe some feelings that you get from imprinted energy.
3. Where can imprinted energy be found?
4. What is a sound imprint?
5. What is an example of a first impression from an energy imprint?

CHAPTER SIX

PSYCHIC SIGHT

You are capable of capturing visual information from beyond the physical limitations of your eyes. This ability is derived from the energy of the human soul. The soul's sight is an extension of the physical sense, and this is why it is a psychic ability. Known by other names such as, the soul's vision, second sight, psychic vision, and *clairvoyance*, psychic sight may be interpreted differently by each person. Clairvoyance has unique characteristics, so one person may experience it slightly differently than another. This is part of your self-discovery. These discoveries help you understand the way clairvoyance works and allows you to determine the "frequency and range" of this natural gift. This chapter explores a variation of the singular psychic sense of clairvoyance and its nuances.

JOURNALING CLAIRVOYANCE AND EXERCISES

Creating a journal with the details of visual experiences can be very helpful in the development and understanding of a clairvoyant sense. This is a personal project and is as individual as a person's personality. The permission that you give yourself in a journal allows you to grow and sometimes heal. There should be no judgment in your private writing; it is just about gathering and interpreting the images received at your third eye. This is where your soul is sensitive to visual energies. The insight gained from any image is valuable because it helps you to develop an understanding about your life and the lives of others. This technique is a healthy way of staying balanced and creating peace around you.

Your journal allows you to review the basic types of clairvoyance. Write down a brief description of experiences related to any of your clairvoyant skills. Below are some questions and areas of interest to ponder while creating a journal. The purpose of this exercise is to identify the area of clairvoyance with which you have the strongest level of impressions. These are exercises for private use and can be used to help you focus. You are then able to attach a particular meaning to the pictures and symbols that you see.

Soul Exercise

1. What pictures or symbols have you seen, and what do they mean?
   _____

2. What past or present happenings have you seen in your mind?
   _____

3. What event do you remember seeing before it happened?
   _____

4. What colors have you seen around someone?
   _____

5. What have you seen with your clairvoyance that was in a distant place?
   _____

6. What information in your dreams had a specific meaning to your everyday life?
   _____

7. What visual experiences have you had that made you feel like you had travelled out of your body?
   _____

8. When and where did you see a spirit's presence?
   _____

9. What other events can you add?
   _____

10. Where were you, and what you were doing when this information came to you?
    _____

Exercises such as these are merely guides to your self-improvement. You can either hide your talents or try to improve them. Images captured by your soul's vision and shown to you in your mind are interesting. If you can learn to recognize the images that come quickly and leave quickly, you can begin to analyze them. Perhaps you can learn to memorize them and associate them with real-time events.

In order to strengthen your abilities, you can study the details in pictures and notice small areas of them. Studying the 1990's cartoon, "Where's Waldo?" is an excellent way to develop your abilities. Finding images in this picture puzzle forces your mind to seek out details and look for specific images.

Exercising your physical sense of sight helps you with your psychic sight by studying details of a received image. The skills you learn with your physical sight can be transferred to the mind's eye. Further, practicing with your mind's eye and imagination is very helpful. When you are imagining a situation, you need to study the details.

Observing with your mind's eye requires the same concentration you would use with your physical eyes, but it allows you to develop your third eye or hidden eye as a muscle. Practicing your clairvoyance creates confidence and trust. Like any other skill, the more you are familiar with its process, the better you are able to use it.

The lines between a "psychic experience" and the imagination may at first seem blurry. A psychic experience is often sudden and unexpected while the use of imagination allows you to drift and go with the flow of a situation. With that being said though, imagination *can* be a channeled event and thus also be "psychic". Furthermore, a psychic movie can have aspects of imagination, but the suddenness from "beyond the physical" is very apparent. Learning the difference will become very clear over time. This practice is an exercise of the soul.

We use our mind's eye and our psychic ability more than we realize. Our mind receives flashes of events, people, and things all of the time. We automatically recognize these pictures and act accordingly. Since it is second nature to us, we do not notice it.

We notice the unusual. The images that we do not recognize or understand are the ones we question. It is frustrating to receive an unfamiliar impression and not know how to react to it. This is when meditation and/or hypnosis can be utilized. These techniques assist us in further focusing on information that we have received and can increase our ability to recognize specific details about an image.

Here's an example. A police officer, familiar with weapons, will be able to identify a specific weapon that flashes before the mind's eye. Another person may be able to discern the image as that of a weapon but will not be able to give specific details about it. The difference is the level of familiarity.

Professional psychics are practiced at recognizing unusual images because they are exposed to many different lifestyles through reading for clients and have gained experience in many areas. This does not make them "omniscient", but they may be able to recognize images of objects or events that a non-practiced person cannot. It means that they are more practiced; that is all. They rely on their experience with images at the third eye to communicate information.

Police departments that use psychics should realize that they do not possess any special powers. They are simply practiced at accepting the information that they receive, and they trust it. The best psychics for police departments many times are the police officers themselves. They are the most experienced with the issues they face. The reason that they may not be able to solve a case can relate to a lot of factors. However, it is best to trust the "flash" image of an experienced police officer when it comes to the areas with which the officer is most familiar. Psychic ability can often give highly trained and experienced individuals a "leap" in their ability to solve a problem. If, however, no progress is being made in a case, a trusted psychic might be employed to move a situation forward or validate concerns.

Observing closely with your physical sight can assist you in developing your clairvoyance since the mechanics of recognition are the same for both types of sight. Remembering the details of a picture or situation that you experienced with your physical sight allows you to recognize those same details when you "see" them with your clairvoyance.

Establishing a "clear vision" and developing the conscious aspect of clairvoyance begins with clearing your mind in meditation. Once you are experienced though, spending a long time in meditation is not as important as it is to the beginner. With practice, you will learn to accept information readily and gain confidence in the images you have received. A clear mind will allow you to "push" your soul's energy or your personal clairvoyant space to envelope another person, room, or area. Clairvoyance can be used long distance with very good results as well.

Pushing out your personal space as an "energy net" allows you to receive energy from another person. Remember, we *are* energy, and we emit and receive energy. Your net can receive visual information from another person which may be sensed in flashes or symbols.

When you receive image information, you must memorize and review the images. Memorizing pictures will allow you to process the information accurately. Practice will remove the need for memorizing because processing will become automatic. Recognition of "what that is" becomes much easier.

Practicing with people who are strangers is very helpful. This is an excellent exercise since there is no prior knowledge about the person.

Clairvoyance is fascinating because a picture is worth a thousand words, and it is satisfying to see the unknown. Many people say, "Seeing is believing." The validation of a visual image removes ambiguity and gives the viewer a certainty of fact. Skepticism has no boundaries, and even a picture can be misinterpreted. Clairvoyance, however, can often be validated with other psychic senses, such as hearing. You might believe something that you hear, for example, even when you do not believe what you see.

Psychic sight has its origins with one's soul, but the body assists the soul with collecting information. Clairvoyance has been known as being associated with the pineal gland of the brain, and scientists are also beginning to acknowledge that inner vision emanates from this area. The pineal gland is located in the center of the brain. It is only about eight millimeters in size, about the size of a pea. In some people, the pineal gland can become calcified due to the intake of fluoride and other minerals. It is an endocrine gland producing melatonin, the hormone that assists us with our wake and sleep patterns. Also, this hormone is known to help us adjust to seasonal patterns of the weather.

In metaphysical circles, the pineal gland is associated with the sixth chakra. This area has other names such as the "third eye" or the "mind's eye". It has been known throughout the ages as the place for mysticism and hidden messages.

Psychic Minute Thirty-One

The mind's eye is located above the eyebrows in the middle of the forehead. This is the area where your soul's vision resides, and it is not associated with your physical vision.

Clairvoyance is an extension of your physical sight, and it exists whether or not you have physical vision. Your imagination uses clairvoyance to give you pictures created by suggestion or inspiration. With your eyes closed, accessing this vision may be accomplished by "looking up" within your mind. With your eyes open, a type of dual vision may exist with your physical and psychic visions. *The physical eyes are the windows of the soul, but the mind's eye is the soul looking out that window.*

Artists use the mind's eye when painting, poets create images for us, we can relax by visualizing peaceful scenes, and we can project where we see ourselves in the future. The uses of the mind's vision are endless, but here, our focus is on the images we capture without trying.

PICTURES, SYMBOLS, AND FRAGMENTS

DEFINITION

As a refresher from earlier in this workbook, clairvoyance, or "clear vision", is defined as *the voluntary and/or involuntary ability of the human soul to access visual information solely within the mind, and it can happen suddenly and without warning.*

This fascinating psychic sense has many variables, and there are several different ways to experience it. It has at least seven variations that the mind uses to provide us with information. These include:

1. Pictures, symbols, and fragments
2. Seeing past, current or future events (premonitions, déjà vu, prophecies, etc.)
3. Auras
4. Remote viewing
5. Dreams (color or black and white)
6. Astral projection
7. Observing spirits

Each of these variations deserves special attention. They are all unique, but they are all visual experiences. We will discuss each of them in detail in this chapter, beginning with "Pictures, symbols, and fragments". The techniques used to study this first variation can be duplicated for each of the other types of clairvoyance.

When you start developing your clairvoyance and notice that pictures or symbols flash in your mind's eye, you need to pause and memorize them. This technique allows you to study the image and discern details that you can save in a "gallery of pictures" in your mind to be accessed for a particular situation or moment in time. A premonition of a lake with trees around it, for example, can be significant for a person who is preparing for a trip. Understanding the details may help give insight about an upcoming event or help avoid problems. The image could also relate to a past event. It might provide details or clues to the circumstances surrounding a mystery.

Soul Exercise

Practice with pictures:

Take a tarot card and flash it quickly, before your eyes forces you to remember detail. Close your eyes and focus on the middle of your forehead just above your eyes. Place the image of the card in your mind and recall the details of it. Open your eyes, write down the details, and look at the card again.

A symbol may be used in much the same way as an image. It can be a signal of a type of recurring event in your life. For example, if a symbol becomes associated with an event such as a visit from a friend or a thunderstorm, "seeing" the symbol may be a precursor to that event. The important message of this exercise is to learn the unique nuances you experience. Your individuality is very much at work when you are noticing clairvoyant moments, and this is true with all of the clairvoyant variances.

Information Fragments

Sometimes we receive psychic images in fragments. At other times, the information streams into our minds like a movie. Most of the time, however, it is difficult to interpret what we have captured. Your body and your soul can be open to receiving the energies of other people and situations, but it is very important that you pay attention. Some people send out information energy better than they receive it, while others are better receivers than they are senders. Psychic abilities, from the perspective of this book, relate more strongly to receiving information than sending it. Additionally, psychic abilities vary, and capturing only a fragment of information is just as valid as having the ability to capture large amounts of it.

PAST, PRESENT AND FUTURE IMPRESSIONS

THE PAST

Psychics see past events around a person. It is the most stable energy. Clairvoyant experiences are more common than people will acknowledge because they do not recognize or accept the fact that the information that they are receiving is "beyond the physical". When we know a person very well and "see" an image around them, we have a tendency to take that information for granted. It is easy to dismiss the image as something that we already knew about them and believe that we are simply remembering. When a total stranger sees a similar image with their clairvoyance, that same information becomes more profound. They know that it is "new" for them, and it is an indication that the energy around the image is very strong. Furthermore, a practiced individual will "see" that information with great detail, and the person receiving the information from them may find it amazing that another person can see accurate pictures of events in their lives. The truth, however, is that the energy from events in our lives creates an imprint that remains with us. Imprints can be sensed and evaluated by those using their psychic abilities.

It is not uncommon to see childhood experiences of an adult when you use your clairvoyance. A person that was an excellent swimmer, for example, may have that energy lingering around them well into their adult years. The imprinted information may not have relevance to current events in a person's life, but that is not the point. It is still a part of their energy.

The point is that the data received about a person's past remains as a point of reference within the total experiences of one's life. Psychic information is just data and, as seen through the eyes of an observer, has no particular or profound meaning. The client is the one that understands its value. As you develop your psychic abilities, your focus is on recognizing visual energy data from around another person and interpreting it accurately. Past energy is the easiest information to see. When this is communicated to a client, it can be a very healing and validating experience for them. Having another person understand their perspective of an event in their lives without any preconceived notions can be very comforting. This is an enormous benefit for someone that may have struggled with their past and has not been able to express their feelings about it. This is especially true when a person has been abused verbally, physically, or sexually. Seeing abuse and recognizing it around another person can bring healing to them. A great weight can be lifted, and issues about shame and guilt released. Understanding another person's pain by "seeing" events in their past validates them and gives them security. A renewed sense of confidence can be gained after this type of critical moment in their life.

Seeing the past can be nuanced like other areas that we have discussed. Severe abuse, for example, can be hidden from your clairvoyant view; however, over time, you can learn to recognize hidden energy. When viewing another person with your clairvoyance and noticing a kind of "shroud" around them, it should be a clue of abuse. Piercing this shroud takes time, meditation, and practice. Once the shroud is pierced, you may be astonished at the things you are observing.

People with deep-seeded issues often forget traumatic moments from the past. They suffer in life by making poor choices with relationships and may seek negative attention without a clear understanding of why they make those choices. While all of us have made bad decisions at times in our lives, a severely abused person can be more susceptible to self-abuse. They are in a unique situation that should be handled carefully.

People handle the emotional scars they have acquired in their lives differently. Some people repeat the abuse they endured upon others, some seek counseling, some ignore the problem, and others block the memories within their subconscious and do not remember the abuse. While these coping mechanisms are not absolute, they are examples of some of the common ways that people deal with their pain.

The reason for discussing the above examples of past traumas is to highlight the dramatic experience that a client may have when their past is seen by another person. The secrets of the past can be revealed by using clairvoyance to see abuse. When an event has occurred in the past, the energy is more stable and, therefore, may be the first thing seen. Past events can even show up as physical characteristics as a result of the extreme energy that they exert on people. In addition, extreme stress can be noticed even when psychic abilities are not used. We can see people have had difficult times by the expressions on their faces. They may look sad or angry or can appear older than their actual age. A psychic reading, however, can illuminate the problems without ever seeing the physical body of a subject. It is the energy around the person that reveals these issues and events.

A clairvoyant reading can validate a person's situation, give insight to solutions, and assist in moving people forward in their lives. It can be very healing and life changing for some. While it is common to notice stress based on a person's demeanor, the details and specificity of the images set psychic abilities and clairvoyance apart from simple evaluation.

For example, a lady came in for a reading and when she sat down, the energy of a trauma was very evident. She did not have to say a word about her ordeal, but the stress and pain of her childhood were evident in the dark shroud surrounding her. Once she acknowledged that she had a great deal of abuse in her childhood, it eased some of the energy around her and the information began to flow freely. She had been the victim of sexual abuse by her grandfather, and she carried a great deal of guilt. The details of the events were vague and difficult to remember, but it was evident, clairvoyantly, that she was the victim of an older man having relations with her. In addition, a younger sister was there as well. It was curious to see a woman in the background that appeared to be in a kitchen washing dishes. She did not appear concerned about events in the other room and continued her chores until she was finished. When her tasks were completed, she went into another room and started watching television. The astonishment of seeing a scene from the past with clarity begged the question, "Why didn't she do something?" The answer was revealed once the focus was turned toward the mysterious woman in the kitchen, the grandmother. Apparently, the lady in the reading had brothers, and her brothers had been subjected to sexual abuse from the grandmother. The perspective that these grandparents had about their grandchildren was that they were "property", and they had the "right" to fondle them. As uncomfortable as it is to discuss the areas of sexual or physical abuse, they are worth noting here because they are examples of extreme energies that alter a person's life. One of the lady's brothers became a sex offender, and his life was changed forever as a result of the abuse that he suffered.

Some other examples of trauma include: accidents, sudden illnesses, and the death of a loved one. In addition, an extremely critical parent, spouse, boss, friend, or sibling can have a lasting negative affect on a person. As all of these can alter the course of a person's life, these energies and events can also be seen clairvoyantly. It is often not pleasant for the "seer" to observe them, but the good it can do for another is enormous.

Fortunately though, seeing the past is not always traumatic. Positive and loving relationships as well as events such as dances, elementary school memories, athletic events, vacations, and many other activities are commonly seen. Happy events and relationships that impact people also leave energy imprints that can be seen clairvoyantly.

THE PRESENT

Present energy, as we are calling it, is the second most stable energy because it is the moment in which we are living, and the energy is "moving". When the energy of someone's present circumstances is high, it can overshadow events from the past. A wedding, divorce, birth of a child, financial problems, or health concerns can be a person's entire focus. Furthermore, relationships and the stresses they bring to people can cause emotional distress that can be seen with clairvoyance.

A psychic sees this energy like episodes in a movie. We start to see how it was generated and where the energy is moving. This movie is like a block in a mosaic. There are many different pictures that can be further examined. If the client does not validate the initial impression of one block, we can move to another. It does not mean that what we see is inaccurate, it may simply mean that we are not able to express the picture correctly, or that the subject wishes to focus on another area of his or her life. We can only see a portion of the present, and it is unsettled. However, if the present information that we give to the client *is* validated by them, we can easily move to possible future events by expanding that particular "movie" and looking further.

Many times, the present energy of a person can be detected in the everyday places you live and work. Standing in the checkout stand of the grocery store or at the mall, you can see images around people. The images can be striking and give perspective about the lives of other people. It is not for you to judge the images and information you see because clairvoyance is often like viewing life through a periscope. The entire perspective of a situation is not understood. It is when you take the time to broaden your view and look elsewhere for data that you gain a better understanding of the person you are viewing.

Another example of a present clairvoyant occurrence is "seeing" illness around people. Noticing diseases that fully encompass an individual is possible due to the stress of the medical condition. Cancer and diseases such as heart disease can be seen as "dots" around someone and can be confusing at times. An individual's clairvoyant mechanism determines the way diseases are seen, but "dots" are one example. Seeing an operation or wounds around a person are other possible indications of existing medical issues.

FUTURE EVENTS

The ability to "see" the future or have a premonition is the biggest expectation of psychics and clairvoyance. This is the type of clear seeing that receives the most attention, but it is the most unreliable form of this ability. It is unreliable because humans have "freedom of choice", and the future can be changed. When "seeing" the future, it must be acknowledged that it is not a certainty that the events seen are going to take place. It is simply the direction in which most of the energy is focused at the moment. *The future you see is "a" future and not "the" future.*

A reading with a woman showed her grieving over the death of her husband's suicide, but during the reading, she said that he was still alive. She had no reason to believe that he was going to die. Shortly thereafter, the lady returned to report that her husband had unexpectedly committed suicide, and she was very upset over it. She was grateful, however, for the information given to her because it assisted her in preparing for the terrible events to come. This dramatic example of seeing the future around a person is not uncommon, but, as it was said earlier, this future was not a certainty. Her husband could have changed his mind.

Another example of seeing the future involved a young man attending a clairvoyant workshop. He saw a boat around me and asked me if I owned a boat. I said, "No," but this did not mean that the vision of the boat was incorrect. There was a ship around me because I was preparing for a cruise within the next month. The problem with the vision was the interpretation. When the "seer" was told, "No," he quickly gave up and felt that he was wrong. He thought it was just his imagination, and his confidence was shattered. When the validation about a ship being in the near future was revealed, his confidence was restored. The problem with placing too much emphasis on interpretation was pointed out and corrected. "Just the facts" are important when using clairvoyance or any other psychic sense. Furthermore, you usually do not have to act quickly when receiving a psychic impression. Time is the most difficult thing to predict; therefore, prudent use of your judgment is necessary. When you see a premonition, you should not overreact.

It is easy to pass judgment and miss the totality of a situation. This is especially true with the future and using psychic ability. Creating fear and misguiding others with your clairvoyance is a real danger when predicting events to come. Seeing "a" future means you are viewing images of the strongest energy at the time. Predicting the future with your clairvoyance is like following a path. There are several paths to most outcomes of a situation, and your psychic abilities pick up the strongest stresses or energies. Sometimes you will see the biggest fears of a person, and it has nothing to do with the correct future outcome. There are limits to your psychic abilities, and to make the assumption that you are omniscient would be a serious error.

The logical question arises, "What value are psychic abilities if they only sense information?" The answer goes back to our original assertions about validating another person's reality, giving them insight, and sensing the strongest possible outcome at the time. These tenants of psychic ability must always be understood to make us most useful to others.

AURAS

Psychic Minute Thirty-Two

The human aura is the electromagnetic field which surrounds the body. The auric field can be sensed by our soul's abilities, and some claim it can be photographed by an aura camera.

The soul's vision is a wonderful gift for us, and the different aspects of it are amazing. We not only have the ability to see events in life, but we can see energy in the form of colors around others. This energy is the human aura, and it is a significant area of clairvoyance. It is very important because it reveals information surrounding a person. The existence of the aura is validated and explained by our psychic senses and by scientific investigation.

The human aura is the electromagnetic field which surrounds the body. The auric field can be sensed by your soul's abilities, and some claim it can be photographed by an aura camera. The aura is a collection of the vibrations our bodies emit, and it is reflected in the various colors of the spectrum. It is interesting to note that our society accepts the notion of auras by depicting them as "halos" around angels and religious figures in pictures. The yellow and white auras seen in pictures indicate the "holy" or special nature of the person they surround and are very familiar and accepted. Since yellow and white suggest "thinking" and highly evolved individuals, it is not surprising that an artist would depict an aura with these colors.

There is a special meaning for every color that is seen around a subject. Auras with a red element in them indicate a person's passions. The meaning of the "reds" ranges from love to great anger. Blues and greens indicate stages and types of spiritual or physical healing around a person. Yellows, browns and oranges mean creativity, grounding, concentration and active thinking. Purple has a spiritual aspect as does a white aura. Darker colors such as grays and black are indications of potentially stressful situations. Living beings emit vibrations that can be detected as colors by your psychic vision, but some people can detect them with psychic senses other than clairvoyance.

As a complement to clairvoyance, the use of your other psychic senses allows you to more accurately understand the precise energy surrounding a person. For example, some "hear" the name of a color when they are around someone. The audio sensation may simply indicate that their clairaudience is stronger than their clairvoyance. Some people "feel" the predominant energy associated with the aura, but never see it. These other psychic impressions are just demonstrations of an individual's soul frequency and range. The point is not to be concerned about which sense you use to examine auras but to follow your own strengths for accuracy.

The vibrations we emit and the colors associated with those vibrations are very revealing since colors represent the types of energies we have around us. Our aura's colors can tell us if we are agitated, pensive, spiritual, stressed, or healing. There are many things going on around us in our lives, and our auras can contain many colors. There is usually one dominant color, but other colors are usually a part of the larger energy field. Most people who see auras see only one color or a small portion of the aura. It is not unusual for another person to see a completely different color around a subject. The reason for this is related to the sensing person's range and frequency of their own soul. Two people can be correct about a subject individual since all of us have several influences affecting us at one time.

The aura is viewed by consciously using your mind's eye to focus on the area just behind the neck of a subject person. It can be seen as a faint image or a glow. Auras can be viewed without any special conditions associated with them, but many people like to have a subject sit in front of a background to assist them during a session. Using your mind's eye to see an aura is a nuance of clairvoyance, and it can give you great insight into a person's life.

When you use your mind's eye, you have several places within it that you can see energy. We have discussed seeing the past, present, future and the existence of a kind of mosaic around a person. The aura is within this mosaic. If the mind's eye was a camera with several different lenses, the ability to see auras would be similar to using a special effects lens. People who say that they have never seen an aura are those who have either never noticed or simply do not have this particular frequency of their soul's energy at their disposal. Since we are all different, it means the inability to see an aura for some people is okay, and those individuals should exercise their souls in other areas to sense information.

There are other means to capture the colors of the aura, but they are controversial. The use of cameras and film to reveal the colors of the electromagnetic field around us is fascinating. Manufacturers of these cameras disagree on the accuracy of their competitors' equipment, and this book is not about whether or not science and technology can capture the true colors of the aura. They do, however, indicate existence of our soul's energy, and the interest in this area by those wanting to demonstrate existence in physical terms is important.

Personal note:

The day my father passed away he had his picture taken. It was not with an aura camera, but there was a strange darkness around him. It may have just been the lighting, but the fact that he died a few hours later was eerie. It was not until I learned more about auras that I noticed this darkness around my father's picture. It made perfect sense to me once I became more metaphysical in my outlook on life.

Exercise

Pick a partner in the room and attempt to see the other person's aura. Use your mind's eye and look just behind your partner's neck. Write down the colors you believe are around them.

_____

_____

REMOTE VIEWING

Psychic Minute Thirty-Three

Remote viewing is the ability to identify information or an object by focusing your clairvoyance on a distant and/or specific location.

It is a part of clairvoyance, but it is also part of another category of psychic abilities that I call the *remote psychic senses*. This sense is the most recognized of the remote psychic senses, and for this reason it is being discussed in this chapter.

Remote viewing is like your other abilities in that there are variations of it. At times, you may concentrate in order to view remotely. Other times, this distant information may just come to you. It is an individual experience, but recognizing visuals beyond your personal space is the common element. Meditation and journaling will assist you in further understanding.

With remote viewing, you are using your abilities to "see" outside of your immediate space, usually over long distances. When done voluntarily, it involves focus and concentration. A mental image of a chosen location is created then the process of observing with your clairvoyance is started. You will then begin to see details. By targeting a thing or place with your mind's eye, you are allowing the information to come to you.

Remote viewing has found a place in our current society and has been practiced by many. There are several groups devoted to developing this skill, and tests have been created to help discover individuals with strong abilities. Organizations, clubs, and other groups all over the world are working on gaining understanding and getting to the next level of development. People are just now investigating the range and nuances of remote viewing. In the future, new techniques and revelations will push mankind to a new level of human consciousness.

Today, you can practice your remote viewing by using the same techniques discussed for developing psychic abilities. The difference is the focus and the targeting of your mind. When you are trying to develop your psychic feelings, for example, you need to clear out all of the feelings you have at the time. The same clearing is needed to develop all of your psychic abilities. Your mind and your energy must be free of the clutter and stresses you have in your life. This is achieved with meditating. Practice will allow you to avoid the dependence of long periods of meditation and give you the opportunity to gather information from "beyond the physical". Trusting is difficult for us, but validation cures this problem over time.

Soul Exercise

Find an item in the news you believe is worth exploring and focus on the issue. Use your remote viewing to gain a greater understanding of an event or a person in the story. You may want to focus on a missing person or a mystery that is unsolved.

_____

_____

It is widely reported that governments, including the United States, have engaged in the use of remote viewing to gather intelligence. The U.S. Government engaged in special projects to develop this skill with significant success from the end of World War II until the 1970's. These programs were suddenly discontinued and discredited later. The work, however, continued in the private sector and remains a popular endeavor for many enthusiasts. The simple task of "targeting" or focusing on objects from the U.S. to Russia, for example, is just an exercise for remote viewing development. The extent, range, and accuracy of it are still unknown. Full understanding is coming, but it is in the future. What was once thought to be unthinkable is now within our grasp.

The applications for remote viewing are endless. However, the opportunity for misuse is great, and there are appropriate and inappropriate uses of it. All psychic skills should be developed with only the best intentions. Still, not everyone adheres to this, and the good done by many can be overshadowed by the evil done by a few. Those who misuse their talents receive an exaggerated amount of attention as a result. However, we also often condemn areas of thoughts and behaviors that are not fully understood. Remote viewing needs understanding and not negative attention.

Example of a Remote Viewing Exercise

Recently, a letter was sent to a popular psychic concerning a missing person. The details have been omitted to preserve anonymity. The letter came from a mother concerning her lost son. Her son was a mentally disabled person who wandered from a lodge in a heavily wooded area. She solicited the assistance of people in the psychic community to find her son. Psychics from all over the country gave their impressions about the situation and reported them to the administrator of the website. The results of those reports were said to be remarkably accurate. The story did not end happily, for with the young man was found deceased not far from where he was last seen. Apparently, he had a heart attack or stroke and was found under some debris that had gathered over him after some time had passed. Many of the psychics contacted, who had reported their findings through remote viewing, had accurately described specific details about the location of the young man's remains. However, they could not say exactly *where* he was located. Clairvoyance is often like looking through a periscope, where there is a narrow view, but not a complete picture.

Other Examples

Popular programs such as "Psychic Detectives" highlight combinations of psychic abilities including remote viewing. The psychics involved often describe places where events occurred with great accuracy. Analyzing these types of programs can provide you with insight into your own abilities and validate your experiences. Practicing with another like-minded individual can be another valuable tool to improve your skills, and this collaboration can help you learn whether or not you are strong in this area.

Soul Exercise

Do this exercise with a friend. Each of you should place an object in your respective homes. Then, each of you attempts to "view" the other's object. Allow the other one to validate the impressions.

_____

_____

Validating impressions enables you to determine your skill level and can build confidence when working with unknown circumstances. If you are not able to pick up the focus objects but can see other objects in the remote place, this is still a validation of remote viewing.

Finally, remote viewing is simply another expression of clairvoyance that has its own unique set of tools. It takes time and patience to understand and develop your personal strength in this area.

DREAMS

When you are asleep and dreaming, your psychic abilities do not rest. The dream state is fertile ground for the development of your skills since it is a period of time when the conscious mind is not collecting and processing information. The unconscious mind takes over and allows you to sort out issues. Your soul is then able to capture information from beyond the physical.

Psychic Minute Thirty-Four

We experience many different kinds of dreams. While a few dreams seem to be only fragments of memories, images, or nonsensical episodes, most dreams have some psychic element to them.
Remember that the reasons we have psychic abilities include: to have an early warning system, to be capable of validating situations that we perceive with our physical senses, and to gain insight. Determining whether or not a dream is psychic can be accomplished by using the journal technique to analyze its relevance to your life based on this definition.

There are different types of psychic dreams. Some of these include symbolic dreams, prophetic dreams, and those that connect us with familiar spirits. These types of dreams may also be recurring and have lessons attached to them. Another experience in our dream state is astral projection. It can take many different forms, not just a dream. (There will be another section below devoted to astral projection.) All of these occurrences can serve you in regaining balance in your life.

Symbolic dreams have metaphors you can understand in your conscious state. Metaphors or stories that you remember from your dreams may not initially appear to have anything to do with your everyday life, but reviewing them may reveal a different perspective. The symbols or stories in the dream may represent an issue you need to address that had not been considered consciously. A recurring dream may give you the same message over and over until the problem is resolved. The symbols may provide insight into previous events as well as represent a future event in your life. You may not understand it until after the event has occurred. In all of these cases, your soul's ability to communicate metaphysically is not diminished with dreams but may actually be enhanced. It simply uses other areas of energy to complete the human experience. Through journaling, you will see patterns over time within your dreams. Your unconscious or subconscious mind communicates with the conscious mind, but unless you pay attention, you will miss the wonderful opportunity to bridge the areas of the soul together. Symbolic dreams are just one type of experience we all have in this special state of sleep.

Prophetic dreams are dreams that contain vivid details about possible future events. They can be intense enough to wake a person suddenly. For example, seeing a damaging storm coming to a familiar area and potentially harming individuals can be very real to a person asleep causing them to react by alerting the conscious mind. Prophetic dreams do not have to be negative though. They can indicate joyous events such as a marriage, the birth of a child, the purchase of a new car or other positive event. The psychic nature of these dreams is identified by their predictive elements. These elements do not necessarily have to be accurate in exact events, but may be predictive or symbolic of a future. For example, a client once came in and talked about her prophetic dreams. She had dreamt that an airplane crashed in a field and that she was there pulling people from the wreckage. A few days later, a commercial airplane crashed. It was not in that field, nor was she there to pull people from the wreckage, but she had still predicted the event. Some people have stronger impressions in their dreams than others. Being disciplined about recording in a dream journal as soon as you wake is a key tool for learning your soul's strength in this area.

A dream dictionary is a good tool to use to interpret and understand your dreams since the experiences of others can provide you with clues about a message contained in a dream. The soul has a language of its own, and it is expressed in our dreams. Used in conjunction with your personal journal, you can "unlock" the hidden messages that are communicated to you through your dreams. There is much to be said about dreams, and these ideas may be the starting point for the exploration of a lifetime.

Dreams can assist you in *communicating with crossed-over loved ones*. These experiences can be very healing or disturbing based on the encounter. Many times, a loved one will appear with a message of resolution, such as saying goodbye if they were unable to do so while they were in the "living". They may want to ask for or give forgiveness in this type of dream. Furthermore, a dream about loved ones may bring additional insight into their lives and give you clues as to why they held certain points of view. Other dreams may give you accurate information about circumstances around an event in their lives such as their last moments. Loved ones may give encouragement, they can help solve issues, serve as guides, or give you "a" future about a path in your life. Generally, the appearance of a loved one is a positive event within a dream. If there is a disturbing aspect, it may be a vivid description of a past event that was not previously known or completely understood. These types of circumstances usually assist with a healing process. A deceased loved one may appear to give you reassurance that they are okay and that grieving for them is part of your path of healing from the loss of their companionship.

Dreams are vehicles for other spirits to visit you in a safe environment. Angels and guides may come to inspire you or give you hope. Their roles vary and usually exist based on your needs at particular times in your life. They are not the final arbiters for decision making, but they can give some insight that you may not have considered otherwise. Angels and guides are around us for many reasons including to provide support and healing with complex or chronic issues. An example of an angel appearing to someone in a dream is the famous Bible story of Joseph, the father of Jesus. An angel came to him and told him not to leave Mary even though he could not be the biological father of her child. Messages from the Divine come to us today through angels and guides. This is why it is so important to acknowledge dreams as a significant part of your life.

Soul Exercise

Please write down a dream you remember and describe details of the symbols or events in it.

_____

_____

A dream during which you believe you have left your body is another clairvoyant experience and referred to as *astral projection*. As with other aspects of psychic ability, this is nuanced and varies from person to person. Astral projections in a dream state may be the most common form of astral projection and is another involuntary aspect of clairvoyance. When you "astral project" in your dreams you will often experience physical sensations resulting from the travel. Waking up tired is a common clue that you have traveled outside of your body during the night.

Astral projection dreams allow you to explore other places, times, or dimensions or enable interaction with spirits. Out-of-body travel does not require a travel agent. It just requires you to pay attention and remember details when possible, just as a person who has traveled to a distant place can remember details and later relate them. You can do the same with astral travel. You can remember the way you felt, the things that you heard, and the things that you saw in one of these episodes. The incident in its totality allows for personal growth.

Sometimes an astral projection dream will take you to a past lifetime, a previous era, or even a historical event. The time travel aspect of this type of dream can be exhilarating because your experience is first hand and without preconception. It is all about your impressions in a moment of time and not anyone else's. Your account is from your perspective alone. Astral projections in the past are common, and traveling to the future is not a problem in a dream state. Visiting other dimensions or alien cultures and consorting with angels, guides, and loved ones are all common events in an astral projection type of dream.

One of the most celebrated examples of this type of dream is from the Charles Dickens classic novel, "A Christmas Story". In this story, Mr. Ebenezer Scrooge was visited by spirits from his past, present, and potential future. His experiences were life altering and changed his perspective about life. Ultimately, he was transformed from a selfish, overbearing individual to a generous, kind-hearted person with empathy for his fellow man. The inspiring story may be a product of the writer's imagination, but it could be based upon the writer's personal knowledge of an astral projection experience.

Thus far, we have discussed involuntary dreams and astral projections. The value of them is to be evaluated in your waking hours after deliberation. Use journals, your memories, and discussion with others to find meaning in them. Astral projection in the conscious state is the next topic as the focus turns to conscious experiences using clairvoyance.

ASTRAL PROJECTION

Astral projections or astral travels, otherwise known as out-of-body experiences, were popularized by the actress Shirley MacLaine several years ago. The public acknowledgement of these experiences validated many people, but it created a great deal of controversy as well. The notion of being able to leave the body and then talk about the experience sounds absurd to the skeptics, but the concept has gained credibility over time. These types of experiences are being recounted by reputable people, and they are being studied by mental health professionals. A therapeutic value is being placed on the idea of astral projection, and Shirley MacLaine has become known as a pioneer in this area of psychic experiences.

We are learning that recording astral projections can give us insight into our psyche and help us to understand our souls' experiences. Answering questions and reliving events that occurred during an astral projection can give us perspectives that may not have been considered by our conscious minds. It is an exercise that our souls use to grow and adapt for our role in this life.

As a part of your clairvoyance, the visual aspect of astral projection deserves attention. It is very common, but like the other areas of psychic abilities, it has variances associated with it such as time travel, traveling to other dimensions, meeting loved ones and guides, or traveling to other places in the present. We have started a discussion about the involuntary types of astral projection in our dreams, but the voluntary aspects are just as compelling. In addition, astral projection has a couple of other nuances not associated with the rest of the psychic abilities. These areas include bilocation of the physical body and the near death experience.

A problem with astral projection is the ability to discern an actual experience from imagination. Your imagination can manufacture a set of events compiled by your mind or given to you by guides. These events are separate from the astral travel experience. Having physical sensations in addition, possibly, to feeling that you are remembering a part of your soul's journey are two critical things that differentiate astral travel from your imagination. A person having an out-of-body excursion may have the sensation of "flying" or moving.

It is common to see people, places or things in other locations in the present, but another aspect of astral projection gives us the opportunity to travel through time. Traveling to the past is frequent and can be experienced on an involuntary basis in your dreams or on a voluntary basis via mediation or hypnosis.

Your psychic journal may be filled with these excursions, giving you a wealth of knowledge that you can use in your life. We call time traveling in the past a "past life regression".

Past life regression is the travel by your soul back to a previous set of experiences. This type of out-of-body journey allows you to gain insight and possibly resolution to situations in your current life. The use of hypnosis can induce an astral projection, and the stimulus of suggestions by a trained professional is helpful in these instances. Furthermore, a person can use self-hypnosis to achieve similar results if necessary, but any type of hypnosis should be exercised with care. In all of the cases, the key element for effective use of the information is to have it recorded.

Projecting in the future is also possible with astral travel, but these experiences are not as well recorded as past life regressions. These precognitive experiences are related to déjà vu moments. A déjà vu experience is one whereby there is the visual sensation of having already experienced a moment in the present.

Finally, "bi-locating" is an aspect of astral projection that is not often discussed. It is beyond the scope of this book to discuss it in depth, but the feeling of the physical body occupying two locations at the same time has been reported. While it is rare, it is worth noting that it does occur. Meditation and hypnosis are tools at your disposal to further develop all of your abilities.

OBSERVING SPIRITS

The last area of discussion for clairvoyance involves the visual recognition of spirits around you. It is nuanced and varied like the other areas because there are involuntary and voluntary occurrences of this phenomenon. However, observing spirits has a very special variation to it in that you can "see" the presence of an entity. Here, you are able to add this physical aspect to the list of ways you can acknowledge presence beyond the physical. While it is often regarded as "just one's imagination", seeing spirits is becoming more accepted by most people.

Another nuance of your clairvoyance allows you to "see" other entities such as aliens from other dimensions. Many people have frequent visitations from aliens, and their presence is distinctive from that of spirit guides or a relative in spirit. Their unusual visual forms and energy emitted are distinct since spirits and aliens have different frequencies. Interpreting these differences is an individual experience, but once a difference is detected, it can be noted and remembered. Other people may not believe in aliens, but once the differences between the two are pointed out, it becomes clear that other beings aside from spirits exist. Acceptance of the reality of alien visitations from other dimensions is becoming more accepted in the metaphysical community. It is another part of your growth and ability to recognize the vast possibilities your soul has to capture information and qualify it.

When you experience viewing a spirit with your eyes, it is a form of "physical clairvoyance", also known as a paranormal experience. The definition of paranormal involves segmenting those events that are beyond the normal explanation of science. Paranormal experiences cover a wide range of unexplained areas such as the physical sightings of unidentified flying objects (UFO's) and unusual creatures like the Loch Ness Monster, mothman, bigfoot, the chupacabras, and others. Our scope is limited to observing spirits and entities which is just one area associated with the paranormal.

Observing spirits is something that cannot be predicted as they materialize on their own. Paranormal investigators have the ability to monitor activity generated by spirits with scientific devices and meters. These instruments validate the existence of the energy that we recognize psychically as spirits. Sometimes, the energy image of spirits is captured by cameras in addition to electromagnetic or EMF meters and can take several forms. Spirits can be viewed in the form of orbs, people, animals, guides or other entities.

Our eyes can see spirits in the form they wish to present to us. Most of the time, a spirit will be seen out of the corners of your eyes and will be there only for a fleeting moment. These experiences are generally involuntary occurrences when spirits want their presence to be acknowledged by you. They are usually friends, relatives, former pets or guides you have known in the past. Since they are familiar, people reporting these instances usually are not afraid when the spirits makes their presence known.

A visitation by a spirit does not have to just be visual, but since this is a discussion of clairvoyance, we are focusing only on this area. Unknown or angry spirits are known to scare people when they are seen. When this happens, it is often considered a "haunting". Hauntings are usually traumatized spirits expressing their anger from experiences that they had when they were in a physical form. Some spirits may be evil entities harassing a particular person during a low period or attempting to disrupt the psyche of an individual. These instances are not the most common experiences we have with spirits, but they need to be noted.

The primary focus of this discussion is on the spirits we see in our mind's eye. Seeing a spirit with your clairvoyance is about noticing a presence that is independently functioning around you or around another person. The spirit portrays an image to which you can relate by indicating that it is a relative, guide, friend, animal or other familiar entity. A spirit's energy allows you to determine whether or not the purpose of the visitation is friendly. We often see a spirit during stressful times in our lives, and they are there to offer us security and the comfort that we are not alone in this life.

Seeing a spirit is usually accompanied by a message as well. Direction or insight may be given, so it is wise to pay attention to these times and accept them as opportunities to learn more about yourself and your situation. Gaining perspective from spirits and having them as a resource can be a good thing, but dependence upon them can be harmful. The sudden involuntary experience of seeing a spirit may be startling at first, but it can alter the course of your life path when a revelation is associated with the visitation.

Spirits can come to you at different times. You do not have to be conscious when a spirit decides to make a visual appearance. They can come to you in your dreams, and you can experience a visitation during a dream astral projection. Hypnosis can assist you in one of these experiences while you are conscious. Furthermore, you can be guided by a medium if you are not able to see spirits around you. This form of assistance is another area becoming more accepted; however, the range and frequency of the person observing the spirits is an area of consideration. Mediums have varying degrees and areas of abilities.

We devote an entire chapter of this book to working with and observing spirits. In that chapter, we explore the use of all of our psychic senses to gain the exact perspective of this phenomenon. Keeping our development segmented is our first focus. Once we have the security of recognizing each psychic sense individually, we can start using them on a more complex basis. It is like learning to use one musical instrument at a time, then creating a symphony once we have mastered our abilities.

Soul Exercise

At this point, let's review the seven types of clairvoyance and briefly write down a memorable experience with one or all of them. This account of your experiences will help you begin a journal for you to keep and identify your clairvoyant skills. A journal will give you discipline and assist you in control of this sense. Please write down in 25 words or less a clairvoyant experience. Note whether or not the experience was voluntary or involuntary.

Type of experience	Voluntary	Involuntary
Pictures, Symbol Fragments		
Past or Present Events		
Prophecies (Future Events)		
Auras		
Remote Viewing		
Dreams (Future or Déjà vu)		
Astral Projections		
Observing Spirits		

While dreams are one of the psychic variations of clairvoyance, there are so many more areas of dreams to discuss. This leads us to the next chapter devoted to a more in-depth look at many types of dreams and their interpretations.

Chapter Review

1. How can journaling assist you in developing clairvoyance?
2. How does your physical sight help you with your clairvoyance?
3. Explain the use of personal space when developing your psychic abilities.
4. What energy is the most stable around a person?
5. What is remote viewing?
6. Name a type of dream.
7. What is astral projection?

CHAPTER SEVEN

DREAMS, THE SOULS' THERAPY

INTRODUCTION

Have you ever had anyone say to you or have you ever said, "I hope all of your dreams come true?" If you have, then you might want to pay close attention to this chapter about dreams and their interpretations. We think about dreams in a positive light, for the most part, because there is a fairy tale aspect to them. A dream is logically thought of in terms of a grand plan of positive wishes coming true. We all want to live happily ever after, and dreams give us an opportunity to do just that. They are part of the imagination process, and it is easy to fantasize about a life with no problems and goodwill for all. The reality of dreams is that they are not about fantasy. They are about the real world placed in terms that are often unrealistic or strange.

You have to learn to interpret your dreams, and a psychic is the perfect person to help you. A psychic's awareness and acceptance of symbols is normal to him or her. Other people may find a dream to be only a bunch of silly impressions that do not mean anything, but the psychic is not so sure. What are the meanings of the images and the story in a dream? Why is this type of information coming to you now? Has this ever happened before? These questions and more leave the psychic searching for meaning.

It should be no surprise to you now that I have the same basic questions to ask you about your dreams just as I asked you about everything else. How does the dream make you feel? What do you see, hear, smell, or taste in the dream? What do you just know about it? Are you keeping your journal and seeing patterns? Answers may come to you once you have completed these exercises, but sometimes a neutral opinion helps. It is becoming more apparent that studying your dreams is a healthy way to gain insight and healing in life. This is just one reason that I say that dreams are the soul's therapy.

The interest in dreams and the search for their meanings is universal. At some time, everyone has experienced dreams that were odd, nonsensical, disturbing, or exhilarating. What are some different types of dreams? Why do we have certain ones? What do they mean? How do we set up a healthy sleeping environment? How do we capture and process the information that we receive from dreams? In this chapter is a discussion of all of these questions and exercises to help you better understand your own dreams.

There are many people who interpret dreams these days, so you will have to navigate through the different methods and find the one that suits you best. Much of this chapter is based upon the findings of other people, and I want to acknowledge their contribution. I have learned a lot about myself by reading and studying the work of others. The internet is a valuable resource that you are encouraged to use along with a dream dictionary for reference.

Psychic Minute Thirty-Five

Dreams occur during periods when the mind is distracted or in a sleep state. They can be the result of the imagination or the brain's natural ability to process information. Dreams are a collection of feelings, images, symbols and/or events. There are several types of dreams, and each has unique aspects.

Dreaming is a natural part of your human experience, and the study of dreams has been around for as long as anyone can remember. Without dreams, the brain would not be able to process information, solve problems, heal from emotional distress, or help you gain perspective regarding current events in your life. Dreams are usually forgotten shortly after you wake, so it is necessary to capture the information you receive quickly. They are experiences that can range from having no meaning at all to being most profound, changing you forever. Some dreams are psychic or prophetic in nature, and these may play a particular role in your life.

SLEEP PATTERNS

The study of sleep patterns is part of dream research. The specific time you are dreaming can be identified within the entire sleep session as REM (Rapid Eye Movement) sleep. Dreaming is a healthy part of the sleep cycle and without dreams, there can be problems with your general health and wellbeing. The lack of dream sleep may be the result of a protein deficiency that needs to be addressed by diet.

Furthermore, studying sleep patterns has helped identify different personality types. Those with short sleep cycles are oftentimes the early risers. They are most productive in the morning with their productivity tapering off during the day. In contrast, "night owls" have longer sleep cycles and tend to be more creative than others. Their energy increases during the day, peaking in the evening hours. Each type of sleeper is equally productive, but their sleep pattern determines whether they are more efficient in the morning or the evening.

SLEEP POSITIONS

It is interesting to note that sleep positions can reveal a lot about your personality in general. For instance, if you sleep on your right side in a fetal position with your hands to your face, you are likely to be a person with a tough exterior and a sensitive interior. You may appear shy in public but will become comfortable once you get to know someone. This is the position in which most women appear to sleep.

If you sleep on your left side in a straight line then you a *log-type* sleeper. You are a sociable person who likes to run with the crowd. People who sleep in this position need to be mindful that they may be gullible in some situations.

Yearned sleepers sleep on their left sides with their arms outstretched. These people have an open nature but have a tendency to be narrow-minded and stubborn at times.

Soldier sleepers sleep on their backs with their arms at their sides. These people are quiet and reserved. They set high standards for themselves and live by them.

The *free-faller* type of sleeper sleeps on his stomach and is generally brash and sensitive to criticism. This person can be arrogant, self-centered, a little gregarious, and can sometimes wear his feelings on his sleeve.

Lastly, *starfish* sleepers sleep on their backs with their arms around their pillows. They are generally open-minded and are good listeners. Being in the limelight is not their ambition, but they can take center-stage when necessary.

It is not uncommon for us to use several of these sleep positions, but we usually have one predominant type we use most often. Also, our personalities are not solely dependent upon the way we sleep since there are a number of factors that can influence us. The types of dreams we experience are varied as well, and they change with our current life circumstances.

YOUR SLEEP ENVIRONMENT

Creating an environment for dreaming and good sleep without distractions is important. A regular time for rest and waking up is part of a healthy lifestyle. Having a comfortable bed in a dark room set at a comfortable temperature is the best condition for a restful sleep with the possibility of peaceful dreaming. Your environment and the stress it can create may cause you to have disruptive sleep and disturbing dreams.

Diet may also be a contributing factor to a healthy night's rest since eating and drinking habits influence sleeping and dreaming. Excessive alcohol, caffeine, heavy foods and eating late in the evening may adversely affect your dreams. When recording your dreams, you need to note these factors, if you remember, to keep any negative information in perspective.

It's good for a sound mind and body to maintain a schedule, eat and drink properly, and have a healthy sleeping environment. While these factors seem to be a matter of common sense, it is not always possible to have ideal conditions. When traveling or during stressful times, you should think ahead to aid with your sleep and improve the probability of "good" dreaming. When out of your normal environment, having additional aids such as ear plugs or an eye mask or taking a hot bath before retiring are tools for a restful sleep. Sometimes, a natural supplement can be used to attain a restful state.

DREAM THEMES

There are often parallels between our sleep styles and our dream themes. For example, if you are a reserved sleeper, you might have dreams about worrying or being cautious. If you have an arrogant sleep personality, you might have dreams in which you bully or are being bullied. Our dreams are generally about us. We are the protagonist in our dreams, and we find ourselves in many different situations. Dreams can be a reflection of the people we are, our personalities, and our perspectives on life. Most often, they reflect the stress we are under during a specific period of time.

Psychologists have different theories for why we have themes in our dreams. The famous psychologist, Carl Jung, supported a theory that dreams have symbols that people share in common. These symbols are universal and are part of an "unconscious collective". The idea of this collective is similar to the concept of the Universal Mind. The Universal Mind suggests that all people on Earth at any point in time in history utilize similar information in their thought processes. This means that the "collective" adapts and uses a higher level of the Universal Mind as man evolves. The symbols evolve as well. For example, a man who lived in the Stone Age may have dreamed about wild animals or weapons. The same man today might have symbols such as cars or cities in his dreams.

Dreams reflect the times we live in and can have a psychic, or prophetic, element to them. They are a reflection of the soul's ability to collect information from "beyond the physical". Your soul's energy field has the ability to obtain information during your waking and sleeping hours. Discovering the frequency and range of your soul's energy is a lifelong endeavor.

TYPES OF DREAMS

1. *Day Dreams*—This type of dream occurs during your conscious hours and involves your imagination. Day dreaming is normal and is usually a distraction from our daily tasks.
2. *Lucid Dreams*—These dreams occur when you are in a semi-conscious state and feel very real as they are happening. You may feel as though you are actually experiencing the events within the dream.
3. *Dreams with Universal or Personal Symbols*—These dreams are ones in which a symbol may appear indicating an upcoming event or situation of which the dreamer has some awareness. It can be an early warning sign and indicates that the dreamer has some precognitive ability.
4. *Visitations from Ancestors, Loved Ones, and Guides*—A visitation from a loved one or a guide may assist you with resolving an issue or enable you to heal from a loss. Angels and guides who come to you in your dreams offer advice and give encouragement.
5. *Recurring Dreams*—A recurring dream is often associated with unresolved issues.

6. *Healing Dreams*—Healing dreams allow you to deal with emotional and physical traumas. During the dream, you are able to dwell on difficulties and resolve them in a safe environment.

7. *Nightmares* —Dreams with frightening situations allow you to face your fears and conquer them. These dreams usually occur during a stressful time or happen as a result of disturbing suggestions before sleeping (ex: watching a horror movie).

8. *Psychic or Prophetic Dreams* —A psychic dream is one with precognitive elements. Familiar symbols in a dream will often show up as signs of future events. An event in a dream can be a warning mechanism for things to come.

9. *Targeted Dreaming*—These dreams are focused on current problems in your life. You can use them to help you work through issues while you sleep.

Exercise

Recall some of your own dreams in the follow categories. Record what you think they meant. On a separate sheet of paper, recount the following dreams:

1. Day Dreams
2. Lucid Dreams
3. Dreams with Universal or Personal Symbols
4. Visitations from Ancestors, Loved Ones, and Guides
5. Recurring Dreams
6. Healing Dreams
7. Nightmares
8. Psychic or Prophetic Dreams
9. Targeted Dreams

DREAM INTERPRETATIONS

When analyzing a dream, you first need to set the dream up by listing the events during the dream. Then, write down the corresponding emotions that you felt at those specific times. This exercise will reveal the most dominant feelings, reflecting current issues in your life. The scenarios of the dreams are generally unusual and may place you in unfamiliar locations or time periods. Sometimes, the dream does not have an ending because the ending is not as important as the journey. When you have a dream to analyze, make a personal assessment of your dreams by asking yourself questions such as:

• What is the overriding emotion in the dream? Fear, anxiety, loss of control, abandonment, lack of safety, trust?

• What are the main issues in my life contributing to these dreams? Problems at home, work, health, a friend, a family member, school?

Soul Exercise

Analyze one of your own recent dreams.

Dream Details:

_____

What is the overriding emotion in the dream?

_____

What type of dream were you experiencing?

_____

Examine possible issues in your life that may have triggered the dream.

_____

What lessons can be learned from your dream?

_____

DREAM JOURNAL

Keeping a dream journal or voice recorder next to your bed is a good way to ensure that you record a dream experience just after waking. The voice recorder will allow you to remember more details, and your voice inflection will allow you to emphasize areas of the dream that were particularly important.

DREAM DICTIONARIES

A dream dictionary is a good resource for a list of symbols, and there are many good ones available to use as a reference. You may be surprised to find you have dreamt about many of the symbols described in them. However, you need to think about the details in your dreams as they pertain to your life. While many types of dreams and their symbols are common, your dreams are still your dreams. Pay attention to what is happening in your life when you try to associate these definitions to your own dreams. The following dream types are some of the more common ones.

DREAM TYPES

Naked Dreams

In the "Naked Dream", the first thing you notice is that you are not wearing any clothing. You must then recognize your surroundings. Are you alone? Are you in a public place? What are the circumstances that you are experiencing at this time? A naked dream may have several different meanings that need to be explored before you make any kind of judgment about it. The following are some examples and interpretations.

Others' Judgement: Vulnerability and fear surround you. It could be that you are in a new job or around new people. A feeling of being defenseless can accompany the sensation of being naked. If you are at work, for example, and know you have an upcoming review, there may be a sense of nakedness around you. You may feel unprepared for a situation that you are facing or may be surprised about the way you are being treated in a given moment.

Shame: You wake up in a crowd and feel everyone is looking at you. The sensation of other people's eyes on you may create a feeling of shame. You may want to find clothing, shelter or just cover up with your hands. You want clothes to help conceal your imperfections and vulnerability. The shame you may feel by your nakedness is because you believe that everyone can see your flaws and nothing is hidden from the scrutiny of others. It is very demoralizing and can cause you to want to retreat from real life situations. During the hours when you are at rest, you can feel safe and allow your insecurities to manifest themselves in unrealistic situations.

Discrimination: Imagine waking up to find that you are in the middle of a football stadium filled with a crowd of spectators. You are naked, and the crowd is reacting to you in an unfriendly manner. How does this make you feel? Where do you go? There is no support for you and it is up to you to handle the situation. It may be the case that the shock of this scene will wake you up.

Insecurity: A naked dream in which your mother-in-law looks at you with an angry face can be very intimidating. In other dreams, you may find yourself jogging naked or engaging in other unusual activities. Naked dreams are usually visual, but you can wake up with just the feelings of shame and "nakedness" around you. These are just as valid and should be recognized when you are making an analysis of your situation at this time. It is a general sense of feeling inadequate.

Confidence: Another dream involving a sense of being naked can involve the opposite of vulnerability. You may feel very confident and unashamed of whom you are. These feelings of being free may be caused by a sense of accomplishment and a sense that you are in control of your life or others around you. This may be the result of a promotion, another achievement, overcoming an obstacle, or some other type of recognition.

Arrogance: Once again, you wake up naked in a crowded football stadium. However, this time, you feel empowered. Instead of embarrassment and shame, you feel happy and hopeful. Instead of covering up, you may stand tall and allow everyone to see you in all of your glory! This is not a moment of defeat. Instead it is a moment of triumph and not caring about the feelings of others.

Making a Statement: This perspective of a naked dream involves a little bit of each of the previous feelings previously discussed. The dream is the result of a desire to draw negative attention to yourself to prove a point, and your actions may be an attempt to embarrass those who see you naked. You may want people to blush or feel like you do not care that they "wronged" you. Imagine our stadium dream again. This time, you may be fully clothed with the audience watching your every move. It may be your decision to disrobe and become naked, or you might just decide to pull down your pants and moon everyone! This act of disrespect to the audience may by your way of being defiant to those around you. A sense of anger that you may not be displaying during your conscious hours may be manifesting in your dreams. You might awaken feeling vindicated for this act of irreverence during your time of rest. These feelings may be satisfied in your dream, and the need to act them out at other times may not be necessary. The privacy of your dream state can prove to be very valuable for many reasons, including resisting a daytime moment you could later regret!

In the case of all of the examples above, your personal examination of feelings and other nuances of the situation may give you the energy you need to move forward in your waking hours. The others around you will notice your confidence, and you may instill confidence in them. These kinds of dreams are not rare and are symbolic of particular events that may be occurring at one time or another.

Chase Dreams

Each dream experience is a learning opportunity for you and can help you with your emotional and psychological well-being. It is essential to pay attention to the messages your soul gives you during your dream state to help you grow. Your psychic development requires you to pay attention to these messages as well.

The chase dream is different from the naked dream because it is a dream about anxiety. It is not about vulnerability or the sense of being free. This is a dream about fears, facing the future, or a particular problem. In this type of dream, you believe that you are in danger because you are being pursued by a perpetrator. This perpetrator may be a wild animal like a lion or bear. It could be a criminal or someone from your past who may have done harm to you. It could be a storm that is making ground on your position and threatening your family, property, or you. The worst fear may come from feeling that YOU are chasing yourself. This could mean that you believe you have unresolved issues that you must deal with, and if you do not, harm is a real possibility.

In these dreams, you may be pursuing a goal or an ideal situation. It may reflect your anxiety that this idea is slipping away or becoming unattainable. The energy in the dream allows you to work out the scenario with specific outcomes. The dream may help prepare you for different outcomes and allow you to deal with the victory or the defeat connected to your goal. When you are trying to analyze this type of dream, you must consider your feelings first and foremost. Your feelings will allow you gauge the level of anxiety you are experiencing at the time. The next area of examination is the visual part of the dream. How far is the danger from you? Is it far or near? The farther away the problem exists the more time you have to prepare for the consequences it may bear upon you. The closer the problem the less time you have to gather your resources to deal with it. If the problem is upon you then you must deal with the issue at this very moment.

Many times this may involve a personal problem that you must face and be observant of your own behavior. Are you acting appropriately? Is there another perspective that you can take? Are you being overly critical of yourself? These questions are ones that your soul may be trying to have you answer. You may be called to look at your situation and decide if your needs are being met.

Write down all of your impressions and determine what meaning you can gather from them. You should be as specific as possible. You may find the answers very revealing as your logical mind is given a window into your unconscious mind. It may surprise you about the insight you are able to obtain from an honest inspection of the dream and your life at this time. Interpreting the experience and using your psychic abilities will allow you to have an 'ah ha' moment which will give you clarity to explain the dream. This is an instance when your perspective is stretched and you have grown.

Test Dreams

If you have ever had anxiety about taking a test in school, then you can relate the emotions that are associated with this type of dream. It is a dream about feeling unprepared or scrutinized. These feelings of anxiety can be met with the energy of motivation or fear of failing. You may believe that the examination by others is unfounded or unfair, and you are trying to make sense of the situation. Often, this is a dream of judgment or the result of being victimized by prejudicial actions by others. This is a dream about your self-esteem, confidence, or not being good enough. You can have these dreams when you are angry with a situation, lack confidence in a given area, are getting ready for a review at work, applying to school, or taking an actual exam. Generally, the people who have these types of dreams do not fail. It is the fear of failure, however, that is dealt with during the dream. Usually, you are very prepared for the upcoming challenge that is being presented, and you can handle the problem.

Examine this dream in the same manner as you have the previous dreams. Write down areas in your life that may be of concern at this time. Notice your feelings and see the situation surrounding the dream. It might be that the test is in another language or something totally foreign to you. This sensation may validate your sense of not being prepared. The lack of a writing instrument could be part of the dream and contribute to a sense of helplessness. The dream may give you the clues you need to be successful and help you prepare intellectually and emotionally for an outcome. If you do not believe you can meet the challenge at this time, it could give insight into ways to withdraw and meet the challenge from a different perspective at another time.

Teeth Dreams

Dreaming allows you to take a peek at life in unusual situations. Dreams about teeth may appear to be strange to the logical mind, but they are very common. These dreams occur when you have feelings of uncertainty. They generally are about the way you feel about your appearance, and it is not unusual to feel unattractive when you are a teenager or going through a change in life. Since losing your teeth is not attractive or comfortable for anyone, the dreams can represent those feelings. When you dream about your teeth falling out, you may lack confidence or have a sense of inadequacy.

However, there are many different interpretations of teeth dreams depending on the details. Some people say that dreaming of teeth can be prophetic, indicating that a pregnancy is around them or that someone is going to pass away. A dream dictionary can be very specific about the different types of dreams involving teeth, so it is good to have one around when you are analyzing dreams.

Falling Dreams

Having a dream in which you are falling is an indication of stress in your life, that you may be feeling a lack of control. Being out of control at work, at home, or because life is not going the way you want, may be reasons for this type of dream. Insecurity and anxiety are common reasons to have a dream with the sensation of falling. It is said that these dreams usually occur shortly after a person falls asleep and can sometimes cause a person to jerk awake to avoid hitting the ground. It is said that this can be part of an arousal system called "myoclonic jerks".

It has been widely thought that if you hit the ground during a falling dream that death is around you. This is not true. Other people believe these dreams can be sexual in nature and may mean you are getting ready to make a gesture to another person involving sexual behavior. A biblical interpretation claims that a falling dream is an indication that a person is not following the ways of God. They are acting along their own belief systems and not those of the Lord.

Examine your feelings and study the situation for insight. You might check your journal for similar dreams in the past. What is going on in your life at this time? What was going on in your life in the past when you had those dreams? Are there similarities?

Flying Dreams

The flying dream is the last one we will discuss at this time. The feelings you experience when you are flying are ones of confidence and self-assuredness. It can be the opposite of the feelings you may have while falling. The two dreams are similar in that there is a sense of being suspended in the air. The difference is the control you have while there.

Flying in a dream allows you to feel free or liberated. If you see mountains and trees, then you may be able to fly over them. The sense of flying over things means that you are able to overcome obstacles and meet challenges. If you are not able to fly over the mountains and trees, it can mean you are not yet ready to meet problems that you are currently facing.

The sense of flying and not being able to maintain flight can mean you do not have the confidence to continue your present course. It can mean there is lack of support in your life and that you may be just keeping up appearances. When you are unable to maintain control, it can be an indication of change, and you are being prepared for a tumble.

A flying dream is part of another category of dreaming. This category is *lucid dreaming*, and this type of dream allows for you to exert some control with your conscious mind. You are an active partner in the scene that is going on around you. It is with this control that you can participate in the outcome of the dream.

There are many lucid dreaming groups who use their experiences to understand their lives better. It remains a matter of opinion whether or not the manipulation of dreams is healthy. Disruption in the normal course of the soul working out issues may prove unwise if not pursued under appropriate conditions.

Psychic Minute Thirty-Six

Psychic abilities are a special part of the human experience, and dreams can help you with your discovery of them. Dreams give you special insight into the ability of your soul to help you overcome issues and are part of your psychic journey to understand life.

Soul Exercise

Following are examples of four different dreams. Use the dream worksheet to analyze each one.

1. A woman had a dream about being in a restaurant and needing to go to the restroom. When she entered the restroom, she checked all of the stalls, but there were no toilets in any of them. This was bewildering to her, and she left without being able to use the restroom.

    Dream Worksheet #1
    Analysis:

    _____

    _____

What is the overriding emotion in the dream?

_____

_____

What type of dream was this person experiencing?

_____

_____

Examine possible issues in that person's life.

    a. _____

    b. _____

    c. _____

What potential lessons can be learned from the dream?

    a. _____

    b. _____

    c. _____

2. A man remembered a dream in which he saw his mother with a look of disgust on her face. He was upset with her because she seemed to disapprove of him.

Dream Worksheet #2
Analysis:

_____

_____

What is the overriding emotion in the dream?

_____

_____

What type of dream was this person experiencing?

_____

_____

Examine possible issues in that person's life.

    a. _____

    b. _____

    c. _____

What potential lessons can be learned from the dream?

    a. _____

    b. _____

    c. _____

3. A person remembered a dream in which they woke up during the night and heard someone breaking into their house. They saw a hand coming in the window.

Dream Worksheet #3
Analysis:

_____

_____

What is the overriding emotion in the dream?

_____

_____

What type of dream was this person experiencing?

_____

_____

Examine possible issues in that person's life.

a. _____

b. _____

c. _____

What potential lessons can be learned from the dream?

a. _____

b. _____

c. _____

4. A woman had a dream about being in a house with many different rooms. An old man would lock her in each room, and she had to figure out how to get out of each room only to be caught again and placed in another room by the old man.

Dream Worksheet #4
Analysis:

_____

_____

What is the overriding emotion in the dream?

_____

_____

What type of dream was this person experiencing?

_____

_____

Examine possible issues in that person's life.

a. _____

b. _____

c. _____

What potential lessons can be learned from the dream?

a. _____

b. _____

c. _____

CONCLUSIONS

Interpreting your dreams can be a disturbing process, especially when the subject of the dream does not make any sense to your logical mind. The symbols and situations presented to us during a dream episode cause us to question and ponder the meanings. You will discover that dreams allow you to face your fears, anxieties, and most difficult areas of your life in a safe environment. Your soul uses dreams to assist you in perfecting your behavior and, as a result, prepares you to meet various situations in your life.

References and Resources:
www.dreammoods.com
www.dreams.com

Chapter Review

6. Why are dreams "the soul's therapy"?
7. What are some factors that contribute to having a good dream environment?
8. Why is a dream journal a good idea?
9. Describe some of the nuances of a naked dream.
10. What is Psychic Minute Thirty-Six?

CHAPTER EIGHT

PSYCHIC HEARING

It never ceases to amaze me about the expressions we use in our everyday experiences and the lack of respect that is given to psychic abilities. We use the phrases like "I heard through the grapevine" or "A little birdie told me." These expressions are often about information we receive through gossip, but other times, they are about receiving verbal information from beyond the physical. Psychic hearing is fascinating to explore and can be a private exercise in the use of the psychic senses.

Clear hearing, or *clairaudience*, is a psychic sense with all of the nuances associated with other psychic abilities but is specifically related to your physical sense of hearing. It is an extension of the physical sense and the ability of the human soul to capture sounds beyond the physical. The area commonly associated with clairaudience is just over or behind the ears. This area is often where you hear a voice not associated with your normal "inner voice" used in daily life, and the ability exists whether or not you have physical hearing.

Recognizing psychic hearing can be accomplished consciously, subconsciously, or involuntarily. When you extend your soul's energy involving this sense, energy from others or a charged situation is captured. This information has not been generated from your logical thinking and could be a word, sound or phrase that is sudden or unexpected. It can be a voice from a spirit guide, crossed-over loved one, or God. Some people regard the ability to hear messages as a gift from God, and thus call it the "Divine ear". Experiencing this type of psychic moment can be life altering and change your perspective.

Example: I believe the first time I recognized the Voice of God was when I was meditating and trying to solve some problems. The voice I heard virtually knocked me out of my chair, and I had to listen. The words I heard were "Be not afraid", the name of a religious song I knew. The moment was compelling and moved me to gain confidence in my situation.

Some use the phrase, "I heard it," to denote the way they arrive at solutions; the answer to a problem or a precognitive message may come through auditory means. That is a clairaudient moment. Hearing a "clear voice" is a matter of paying attention and trusting the information received. Your usual techniques; meditating, identifying your personal hearing space, paying attention to words you hear, and practice are essential elements in your clairaudient development.

Clairaudience is not easy for many people because this sense requires patience. It has variations that include hearing specific voices from crossed-over loved ones, guides, and angels. Learning the difference takes time, and trusting the voices you hear is a matter of your personal judgment. The voice of loved one may resonate more closely with you than that of a guide or angel. By distinguishing the different frequencies of the voices, you can determine what type of spirit is talking to you. Another way to determine this is by the expressions they use. A loved one may use familiar terms, an angel may use more flowery words, and a guide might give advice. This is the mediumship aspect.

Clairaudience can range from hearing, "You left the coffee pot on," to, "I am still with you," from a loved one. Hearing words with a special meaning to you can be a very moving and emotional experience. As a result, learning to use clairaudience can be a powerful tool for your life. Musicians and other types of artists hear creative inspirations with their clairaudience. Entire symphonies, for example, are heard first with this ability before they are committed to paper.

Psychic Minute Thirty-Seven

Using the soul's ability to capture words or advice is called a "mantra".

Meditating on an event or situation may allow you to receive key words. A "mantra" from a guide or an angel working with you can give you an edge when dealing with someone or something. You may hear, "Stay calm," for example, compelling you to remain composed in a potentially volatile situation. An opposite mantra could be equally useful. Either way, you will have an edge; not to mention, the comfort that *you are not alone*.

Soul Exercise

Meditate on voices you hear to help you identify them. Note any you *hear* below:

Loved one-The sound of a loved one in spirit can be identified by the tone of the voice and/or the expressions used by them while they were in the physical world.

_____

_____

Guides—They generally speak metaphorically or with symbols. Guides will come to you to support you in areas where you need encouragement. Wisdom, joy, or compassion guides are often those who contact us.

_____

_____

Angels—They are often inspirational and are recognized by their special tone and the information they give. The archangels can play a large part in your life and can appear by themselves or with other angels. Angels who channel through you will often appear to you in groups of three, five or seven. You may notice more than one voice if you are a writer, songwriter or other type of artist as angels often direct our work. Angels who channel through you are usually "all business".

NUANCES OF CLAIRAUDIENCE

Psychic Minute Thirty-Eight

As with the other psychic senses, clairaudience has nuances associated with it. These include active prayer, "direct voice", and hearing the thoughts of another person.

Active Prayer

When we pray, we are generally petitioning God to grant us something. Formal prayer is when we use a written text as a means of communication with the Divine. The hope is that answers will be given to us. One of the practices with prayer is to listen. Praying and listening for answers is part of the Christian faith. The voice of God is credited by many as the reason for taking action in their lives. Many preachers on television recount hearing God's voice giving them direction to preach His Word. This is an unrecognized occurrence of clairaudience but a perfect example of an instance when it is present.

Direct Voice

The second nuance is the direct voice. This is the voice you hear with your physical ear, but it seems to come from nowhere. It is a phenomenon from the spiritual world. It can come from a crossed-over relative or spirit guide to simply give you confirmation that the spiritual realm exists and for no other reason. However, a direct voice can have an important impact on you if you are seeking confirmation or direction in your life. This is a connecting with spirit instance and an experience "beyond the physical".

Hearing Thoughts of Others

The final nuance of clairaudience involves hearing the thoughts of another person. While it is called "mind reading", it is a clairaudient experience. You may be standing next to a person and suddenly hear talking. However, they are not talking, nor is there anyone else nearby. This can be associated with a "cool breeze" feeling touching you. The thoughts you hear are current and may involve issues a person is attempting to solve or just their mind chatter. This ability may not happen all of the time but may be frequent enough to recognize it as a "beyond the physical" experience. You should use discretion if you recognize that you are sensing the thoughts of another person.

MORE SIMILARITIES TO THE OTHER PSYCHIC SENSES

As with the other psychic senses, when you understand the way clairaudience works with you, you will acknowledge different sounds as an alarm or a premonition of an upcoming event. A bell, for instance, may be heard before the phone rings. The sound of a person's voice may be heard before they enter a room. Some sounds may indicate that a stressful encounter will follow or that danger is near. You must learn to recognize the clairaudient signals that your soul sends to you since *everyone is different.*

The ability to use psychic hearing compliments your other senses. We are energy beings, and the possibilities of your psychic development is not limited to just your feelings, sight, and hearing. Pushing the limits of your human experiences allows you to explore other possibilities for your soul's energy to work. Psychic abilities have their own characteristics. If you recognize some gifts, you will usually have all of them present to some degree.

Soul Exercise

1. Recognizing Voices—Notice fragments of words and the tones of the voices you hear. Keep in mind that there are healthy and unhealthy voices in our heads. Healthy voices will never make destructive suggestions. Note a time when you can remember hearing voices.

    _____

    _____

2. Validation—Can you recall when you heard voices and later found that you learned in advance something that you otherwise would not have known?

    _____

    _____

3. Make an inventory of sounds—Listen to the sounds of nature either outdoors or on a nature recording.

Soul Meditation #5

Go to your sacred space and take at least thirty minutes to pay attention to your psychic hearing. Use this time to call upon your loved ones and guides to communicate with you. Notice the difference between the sounds of the physical world and the sounds coming to your from beyond the physical.

Develop knowledge of sounds as symbols from your psychic sense of hearing. Begin to notice them for their precognitive nature or for the increase in your perception.

Review of Chapter

Define clairaudience with the information you have read in this chapter. How do you use clairaudience with the rest of your abilities?

Continue to practice and pay attention to the sounds around you. Identify those sounds that are acceptable by your physical senses and those received by your extended sense of hearing.

CHAPTER NINE

PSYCHIC TASTE AND SMELL

Psychic impressions strike you when you least expect them. The soul is always aware of energy, and the extended senses of taste and smell might be the most unusual of all of the abilities. Many times, pregnant women have cravings for particular kinds of food, or you may want to eat foods indicating the need for a particular mineral. Your physical body communicates with you for these needs, and you should pay attention to them. Whereas the physical can be associated with urges and 'hankerings', your extended senses can also give you sensations from beyond the physical. The true psychic notices the differences. This chapter should assist you in determining these differences along with practice.

CLAIRGUSTANCE

The sense of psychic taste, or clairgustance, is the recognition of a particular taste sensation in your mouth without any explanation of the origin. The soul's energy that is sensitive to this energy corresponds with the body as with the other senses. It can occur suddenly and for no apparent reason. Again, like the other senses, psychic tastes may be captured consciously, subconsciously or involuntarily. Many people are able to capture thee tastes, but they do not recognize them as metaphysical senses. It is not until they review different circumstances in their lives that they are able to make the association. Note that the expression, "I can already taste it" usually refers to an imaginative taste that may be real but not psychic. It is important to make the distinction.

Psychic Minute Thirty-Nine

Clairgustance should not be confused with a heightened sense of taste.
Some people naturally have enhanced tasting abilities. Again, this is different from psychic taste. Those with a heightened sense of taste often become taste testers or wine tasters, for example.

Expanding your perspective is important when developing your psychic skills. A psychic taste experience could be linked to statements such as, "I just had a sudden taste in my mouth." The unusual occurrences of these tastes indicate the psychic element, and the capability to validate an event with a good or bad taste in your mouth is a symptom of the ability.

Soul Exercise

Have you ever noticed a taste in your mouth that served as a first impression (positive or negative) about an individual or situation? Recount the experience.

_____

_____

Recount an instance when you said, "I have a foul taste in my mouth," and the unpleasant flavor validated a problematic situation.

_____

_____

Recall a situation when you might have said, "I can just taste it."

_____

_____

Psychic Minute Forty

Psychic taste can enable you to recognize a spirit around you.

The taste of a favorite relative's pie or fried chicken can be an indication of their presence. It can be a signal you are receiving a visit from them for communication with taste is more common than you might think.

Developing your psychic taste is much like the exercises described for developing your psychic feelings. Meditation and clearing your mind with the intent of discovering the tastes of different foods or recognizing the presence of a particular taste when similar events arise will give you clues about the way to use this ability in your life.

Dwelling on different tastes will allow you to notice different characteristics of a sensation. For instance, your grandmother's apple pie may taste different than your aunt's. That difference may be important when identifying a particular spirit visiting you. These subtleties may have to be experienced. If your aunt and grandmother used different spices, that can be your clue. And, if you have a relative who had a tendency to burn things, that can be significant! Learning your taste bud sensitivities allows you to be very accurate in describing a particular psychic moment.

The psychic sense of taste also has a remote quality that is similar to the other beyond the physical abilities. The idea of remote taste is not generally recognized but may exist with some individuals.

Psychic Minute Forty-One

It is often noted that the psychic sense of smell and taste are used together as one. Furthermore, it works with our other psychic senses to alert us.

Even if you are not as comfortable with clairgustance, it is often the immediate recognition of a taste sensation that triggers another sense that you can identify. The taste may serve as a catalyst to open your other psychic senses, and one of these senses may be easier to understand. This is another individual tendency that you will experience and learn to recognize over time. You should be patient with clairgustance development, for it is often not associated with a psychic skill like psychic feelings, clairvoyance or intuition. People who use psychic taste as their primary source of "beyond the physical" abilities are usually the ones who keep the information to themselves.

Soul Exercise

Recall any tastes that allowed you to notice an aroma, feel an emotion, have visions, or just know answers to problems.

_____

_____

Physically taste several flavors to use as a reference when you experience a "psychic taste."

Soul Meditation #6

Dwell on flavors you know and remember them for future reference when a psychic impression is present. Developing your inventory of tastes will assist you in your development. Dwell on situations with your conscious mind and determine if you can taste something at a given event.

Journal

Journaling your experiences with this ability will assist you in recognizing when particular tastes are present. It will give you clues when to expect these flavors when they appear on a sudden basis without anything in your mouth.

Practice With Your Soul's Energy

Close your eyes and identify flavors.

CLAIRFRAGRANCE

The other psychic sense we need to discuss in detail is the ability to capture scents. While *psychic smell* is the term commonly used in the metaphysical arena, clear smelling can also be known as clairfragrance, clairolfactory, clairscent, or clairaroma. The definition of psychic smell is essentially the same as the other psychic ability definitions. It is the human quality to capture scents beyond the physical limitations of the olfactory glands. The area just beyond the nose is where the soul receives the energy information. This ability, powered by the soul, can be used consciously, unconsciously, subconsciously, and on an involuntary basis. Capturing scents, recognizing them, and being able to act appropriately when they are received requires patience and practice.

We often use terms such as the **smell of danger** or the **sweet smell of success**. These particular expressions may not appear to some people as psychic but there is a beyond the physical element associated with them. A precognitive odor that is positive may give you confidence to proceed with pursuing a wanted outcome. On the other hand, if you receive a negative sense before an event, you may choose to withdraw or take precautions to offset a negative outcome.

Your nose can detect scents on a psychic level, and it can also notice smells directly associated with spirits.

Psychic Minute Forty-Two

Psychic smell can make you aware of a spirit around you.
Dwelling on various familiar scents may assist you in identifying spirits. You may notice the scent of a powder associated with a deceased mother or grandmother. The smell of pipe tobacco or the smell of a man's cologne may indicate the presence of a father, grandfather or another man in spirit. There are many other smells that may remind you of someone, indicating their presence. Furthermore, a foul odor may be a clue to difficult times ahead.

Soul Exercise

Do you recall an instance when you experienced a sudden smell that reminded you of a crossed-over loved one?

_____

_____

One aspect, unique to the sense of psychic smell, is the ability to smell disease. People are beginning to accept the idea that dogs are capable of recognizing illnesses and can be trained to alert us. However, some humans have this ability as well. We normally do not think of a disease as having an odor, but diseases such as cancer have a distinctive foul odor to those with psychic smell. Once recognized, this ability can be a valuable tool. It may be helpful to the medical profession as well if there are any physical attributes that can be identified.

Common expressions may be used to describe psychic smells. While these same comments may be used casually, simply as a negative description, there are times when they are used in conjunction with a non-physical aroma. The term "this stinks" can be a psychic expression when there is no apparent physical scent. In other words, a situation has a stench when is not good, and the energy is foul. Some people may detect an offensive odor when facing a problem or a stressful situation. If the expression, "I smell a rat", is used when there is no logical reason for the comment, then there may be an underlying "beyond the physical" explanation. Again, while often used *only* as expressions, these statements can sometimes have a metaphysical connotation worth noting.

Psychic Minute Forty-Three

You may become more aware of your surroundings from your psychic sense of smell.

Capturing the energy of an odor that does not exist in physical form may validate an upcoming danger or that a person of significance is near. This sense can open the door for your other psychic senses and cause you to put your other physical senses on alert.

Soul Exercise

Do you recall a sudden smell (good or bad) that was later validated by an event?

_____

_____

Psychic Minute Forty-Four

Clairfragrance should not be confused with a heightened sense of smell.

With clairfragrance, there is no physical odor or stimulus. Some people simply have a heightened sense of smell. People who choose to be perfume testers, for example, are able to distinguish scents with a great deal of accuracy. They are known as "noses".

Psychic Minute Forty-Five

As with the other psychic senses, psychic smell also has remote components.

There are times when odors come from a distance. Information can be received with uncanny accuracy but often goes unrecorded and unrecognized as a psychic event.

Anticipation

Psychic experiences need to be separated from the concept of anticipation. Anticipation is a conduced response by the logical mind. You can imagine a feeling, vision, thought, voice, taste, or smell. However, it is the sudden unexpected nature of psychic abilities we are addressing. Recognizing the type of sensation you are experiencing and knowing that it is psychic allows you to know that your soul is working with you in a very special way. Nevertheless, anticipation can be a good tool to assist you with your development. Studying the various nuances of your personal perspectives allows you to recognize them when they are not manufactured.

Developing inventories of sensations is a necessity if one is to be well practiced. The more you are engaged in an activity, the more you can anticipate data. This is true with regard to your psychic ability in any area of discipline. You know whether the energy around you is positive or negative. Everything may have the appearance of perfection, but your psychic senses will let you know otherwise.

Soul Exercise

Use your physical sense of smell to recount positive and negative odors.

Soul Meditation #7

Consciously focus on smells.
Unconsciously receive smells and recognize them with your conscious mind.

Journal

Use the same techniques you employed when journaling your other soul experiences with your psychic taste to assist you in recognizing when particular smells are present. It will give you clues when to expect these scents when they appear on a sudden basis without a physical odor.

Soul Practice

Close your eyes and identify odors. Make your own personal inventory of smells.
The next chapter continues the development of our sensitivities to a singular ability by focusing on the next psychic sense, intuition. This topic shifts our attention to the mind, and therefore shifts our perspective.

Review

This brief chapter requires more study and practice for some people because it is not as evident that these senses are as active as the others. Use your journal to record your experiences and learn about the taste and smell sensations coming to you.

CHAPTER TEN

PSYCHIC KNOWING, INTUITION

Einstein may have said it best, "Intuition is everything." I believe he meant to use the word intuition as a substitute for all of the psychic senses. However, this chapter is specific to the psychic sense known for 'knowing something' from beyond the physical. The 'knowing sense' can be the most difficult and, at the same time, simplest of all of the senses to investigate. It is so natural that skeptics will dismiss it as coincidence, but the psychic takes nothing for granted. You should not either because your soul is the energy that you use to capture or acquire information not readily 'knowable' to you.

It is important to develop a foundation before starting to explore psychic skills. The foundation involves taking stock of previous experiences and understanding the way information is accessed. The psychic information might just "show up", but it is good to sort out whether the information is visual, emotional, or "just knowing".

Intuition, or claircognizance, is a unique form of psychic ability and is not associated with a feature of the body like the eyes or ears. (For our purposes, I will use *intuition* as a substitute term for *claircognizance*.) Intuition involves the mind. The mind is always at work, and we think continuously, even as we gather information from our senses. When we are involved in an activity, our minds are fully engaged. The sudden introduction of an idea about a problem or a situation is associated with intuition. Information coming to us in this "just knowing" form does not involve any work, and we have difficulty recognizing that which was not created from logic or imagination.

Having faith and trust in information received intuitively is difficult. A psychic has to take chances and communicate ideas that drop into their minds even when they appear to be fantastic or unbelievable. We tend to dismiss our intuitions and to ignore our access to energies. If we do not have confidence, faith, and support from others, we will never be able to develop our abilities. Most people keep their psychic impressions private because they doubt themselves.

PSYCHIC MINUTE FORTY-SIX

Learning to use your psychic ability is not a competition.
People have varying degrees of abilities, and these skills may be present in a variety of different areas. As I have said before, learning to develop them is not a competition but an

effort to understand ourselves. You may have a strong sense of intuition, but you may lack the other abilities commonly associated with being psychic. This is okay since the wise use of any or all of the extended senses should be a positive and fulfilling experience in your life. This chapter expands on the ideas introduced in Chapter One.

Why Do You Have Intuition?

I would like to return to one of the original Psychic minutes for the explanation: *Intuition is given to you for the same reasons you have psychic ability in general; 1) it serves as an early warning system for an unforeseen event or events, 2) it validates your cognitive abilities, and 3) it gives insight or solutions to issues in your life.*

Early Warning

If you review some of your experiences, you may be surprised at the many times you have used intuition in your life. How many times have you heard someone say, "I knew that was going to happen"? There is no explanation as to why people have this information, but it causes us to reflect and try to understand the mechanics of our personal predictions.

Validation

You may receive information from your logical impressions then suddenly have an impression that comes metaphysically to validate an assumption. This validation is a psychic impression that you can act upon, but you would not have made the connection unless you had allowed your physical senses to experience the situation first.

Insight

An insight or a solution to a problem may be presented to you without looking for it. It simply arrives on its own and cannot be explained. A concise definition of intuition is an elusive one, but the following one will assist you in understanding it. "Intuition is the human soul's quality to consciously, subconsciously, or involuntarily receive "thought" information beyond the limitations of the mind."

Intuition Involves the Mind

The term, intuition, is used generically and is often confused with the other psychic senses. However, the principal ability involves the mind and your thinking, and the other psychic senses may be "door openers" for your intuition. The other senses allow your intuition to be stimulated, but it is a thought "dropping into your mind" that allows you to have a "knowing" about a person, event, or situation.

Since intuition involves your mind thoughts, it may be the most evolved form of psychic ability. Very intelligent people throughout history have demonstrated strong intuitive gifts.

They have allowed their abilities to give them insight into problems that have moved mankind forward with new ideas.

Our goal here is to narrowly define intuition to *thought beyond the limitations of the mind.* As the definition is meant to be used as a guide, you can use the term in whatever way you are comfortable. Information is received at many levels, but it is the *knowing* aspect of this gift that makes it unique. Meditating, clearing your mind and emotions, discovering your personal space, and expanding your thoughts to a person, event, or situation will allow you to gain insight. The insight might simply be a word, an invention, a creative endeavor, a new approach, or another unique idea.

Practicing how intuition works with you can be accomplished with puzzle exercises, video games, or playing charades. Playing card games involves skill, but a little intuition can be the "edge" you need to be successful. Paying attention, observing behavior, and trusting information are key to understanding the way intuition works for you. When a thought or answer falls into your mind, you will understand that this is intuition at work.

Intuition is another powerful tool for you to use as you develop your psychic skills. It is part of "putting it all together" and understanding your abilities. Moving forward, you will use these skills for mediumship and channeling.

Recognizing Intuition...The Mechanism

The first part of learning how to use your intuition is recognizing it. The sudden thought that strikes you without provocation and the solution to a problem in your life that simply appears as a thought are both examples of intuitive moments. The "knowing" you have with regard to a person or a situation is also important to notice.

Your intuition is used interchangeably with your normal thought processes, and the difference between the two is that intuition is not logical. A logical approach to a problem follows patterns, procedures, investigations, designs, and/or formulas. Intuition is the inspiration or hunch that is unexpected and not explained.

Intuition on a grand scale...The Universal Mind

The soul captures energy in many ways. We need to acknowledge the symphony of all of the psychic senses working together while understanding that intuition has singular qualities. The other psychic senses operate slightly differently from intuition. While intuition can serve as a catalyst in the activation of other psychic senses, the reverse of this also occurs. One of the ways intuition captures information is "The Universal Mind". The other psychic senses can be door openers for intuition, and the soul is capable of using these senses interchangeably. Furthermore, not only is intuition unique for every person, but there are situations when it is not limited to the individual's senses. Human beings are connected and share the same kind of energy from their souls. This energy reaches out beyond our physical experiences and captures information. The wonder of our spiritual nature allows us to act as a collective and journey together as a species.

Intuition is innovative and progressive. It can be the inspiration for formulas, theories, and the like; however, it should not be surprising that intuition is independent of any norms. Sudden new ideas can be obtained at virtually the same times in different parts of the world, allowing man to collectively progress along similar paths without reference to each other. Therefore, this psychic ability can be linked to the concept of the Universal Mind, often referred to as the "Hive Mind".

It is not unusual for the scientific community to use a "kind of" Universal Mind to prove concepts. The common practice of allowing different laboratories to research and solve similar problems follows this idea. If one lab resolves a scientific issue and another lab solves the same issue about the same time, then the scientific community is more apt to accept the solution. Of course, further studies follow, but the discovery remains an example of the Universal Mind and Intuition.

A notable example of tapping into the Universal Mind was the development of atomic power. Several countries were simultaneously working on the concept during World War II. While the United States was the first to capture a practical application, once only in the Universal Mind, scientists from around the world were drawing similar conclusions from the same energy independently. Information from the Universal Mind often first presents itself as theory until it is filtered down to us.

Other examples of intuition and the Universal Mind include the development of the automobile, electrical energy, and the airplane. Examples such as these can be sited during each age of human civilization. Periods in our history such as the Iron Age, Bronze Age, Renaissance, and others hold creations, inventions, and progress that point to the use of the Universal Mind.

The Universal Mind is a phenomenon that has been discussed since the early days of philosophical thought. The ancients talked about the idea stating, "We are all one." Not only has the idea of the Universal Mind evolved over time, but it can also be suggested that the Universal Mind itself evolves and changes. It remains at least one step ahead of the human experience.

Mankind moves forward "capturing" and understanding information received from the Universal Mind. Our mental and spiritual growth comes from comprehending this information, but is important to note that the Universal Mind is not God. It is only one aspect of God because God is greater than just the Universal Mind. Our ontological proof of God remains valid, and God remains greater than anything we can conceive.

One analogy describes the idea of the Universal Mind as that of a tornado with a tail growing larger and larger as it moves towards the sky. Mankind has tapped into the tail of the tornado over the course of history, but because the tail was narrow at the bottom, the growth of new ideas had not advanced very far until the last hundred years or so. That was when man started to move forward with new technology to simplify his life on this planet. In more recent years, mankind has tapped into larger areas of the tail or funnel of the Universal Mind tornado. We are moving forward at an exponential rate these days as we see technology advance very quickly. Advancements once took centuries, then decades. Later, change took years, then months, and now it sometimes takes days or hours for advancements to reach the public. It is fascinating, the ability of mankind to capture and realize new ideas at an ever faster pace. We can only imagine the amount of advancement mankind will make in the next ten years.

The concept of the Universal Mind is controversial, but it needs to be discussed in terms of the human experience. We can imagine that tornado described in the above analogy. This is a simple image of the Universal Mind and human history. Mankind has evolved intellectually over the centuries by reaching into the funnel. Reaching upward into the Universal Mind has pushed mankind forward. The Mind is nuanced, with certain periods of history progressing faster than other times. The Dark Ages, for example, were times when people were either not allowed to express themselves or were not paying attention to the upward energy of the Universal Mind. When politics and conditions eased for people, inventions and innovations resumed, and the human race began to move forward again.

Today, we are in a larger part of the funnel of the Mind. This provides an explanation as to why we are moving forward with technology at such a rapid rate, and the quality of life of our species is improving exponentially. It is the capturing of information from the Universal Mind that is allowing us to move in a positive direction. Intuition is a mechanism we are using to obtain and control this information.

The Universal Mind and intuition have changed our lives and society forever. The idea of the "tornado" with the funnel growing ever larger toward the top is just one concept. There are other schools of thought that describe the universal consciousness. The ancients introduced the idea of one consciousness and the concept of a "hive" mind. Imagine a bee hive buzzing with activity and all of the participants in it playing a part to help the hive survive. This is like everyone on the planet "buzzing" and sustaining mankind on its journey through the ages.

The Universal Mind has subcomponents or various "hives" to it. These components or "hives" can be broken down into geographic areas, nationalities, races, groups, companies, professions, religions, political persuasions, teams and even families. It can be argued that, when one member of a "hive" draws a conclusion or experiences an intuitive moment, several other members of the "hive" can have the same experience. This is because their soul's energy can capture information resonating from the "hive" energy.

Intuitive links between people are very common. It would be unusual for a person not to have experienced reaching a conclusion at the same moment as another person within a group of souls. While this ability is not limited to people within a community, it is most common with people of like interests.

Have you ever simultaneously reached the same conclusion as another person when solving a problem? If you have, you may have considered it a coincidence. However, upon further reflection, you may realize that you were connected spiritually to your "mental" counterpart. It is not uncommon for friends and foes to reach similar conclusions based on their mutual connections to a similar hive of the Universal Mind.

Soul Exercise

Have you ever reached the same conclusion for a problem simultaneously with another person?

_____

_____

ENERGY OF THE SOUL

Psychic Minute Forty-Seven

The mechanism of intuition has unique qualities but they all are derived from the energy of the soul.

ALL psychic ability is derived from the energy of the soul and the Divine. Each psychic sense is associated with a particular part of the body, and intuition is no different. Clairvoyance corresponds to the area on our foreheads just over our eyebrows, clairaudience is noticed at the area above our ears, and intuition is known to be at the top of our heads. It is in this place we feel thoughts drop into our minds.

The soul is energy, and it surrounds our bodies. It emits and receives energy and information from the universe. This energy is in the form of strings and, if seen, would appear like electrons surrounding the nucleus of an atom. When we are not under stress or working on a problem, the energy around the soul is balanced. However, stress and problems create an imbalance around us. This is when we can "capture" energy from the universe to assist us with healing or solving a problem. However, while pondering a problem, we attract both positive and negative energy from the universe. What we attract holds the key to our peril or the answers to our questions.

If you pay attention and stay open to receiving answers, they can drop into your mind. Emitting positive energy allows you to attract answers and gain the knowledge needed to move forward. With a positive attitude, you can learn to attract answers. Creating this positive energy can be done with prayer, meditation, and the support of others.

THE GENIUS THEORY

Psychic Minute Forty-Eight

The use of the gift of intuition is used by the most intelligent people thus creating a Genius Theory.

Albert Einstein said, "The only real valuable thing is intuition." It is not surprising that he was complementary of intuition since he was one of the greatest geniuses the world has ever known. This man recognized that he did not "manufacture" answers to the great issues he attempted to solve. The answers came to him from another source. Einstein was simply open to receiving information.

Successful people are very "intuitive". These individuals may or may not have other qualities to which they can attribute their good fortune. However, they just seem know the right direction to follow. It is possible that they have a different soul frequency that allows them to capture more energy from the Universal Mind, but they are also more likely to act on that information. It is important for us to understand that we must not only recognize energy, but we must also be able to articulate what we grasp.

This does not mean everyone will be financially independent, but it does mean that paying attention to signals, information, and other sensations can lead us in very positive directions. Many very simple individuals are successful because they trust their "intuition" and remain steady on a course.

Soul Exercise

Have you or a person around you been called a genius based on a knack for creative and/or original ideas?

_____

_____

WOMEN'S INTUITION

Psychic Minute Forty-Nine

The expression, women's intuition, is a term commonly used by our society to acknowledge the uncanny accuracy of many women to innately have answers to problems or to make predictions.

While this gift is called *intuition*, it is really a combination of psychic abilities. It is often described using terms associated with other psychic gifts such as *feeling*, which refers to clairsentience, *vision*, which refers to clairvoyance, and *hearing*, which refers to clairaudience. It is the *just knowing* or sudden thought that is attributed to intuition.

Psychic touch is another element involved with a woman's ability to understand situations. When women hold children, they use their ability to capture information by sensing the child's energy through touch. Furthermore, extending their energy from their personal space allows them to be "in tune" with their child when they are not holding them.

Society is suspect of people when they say that they are psychic. However, people are refreshingly silent when a woman says she "just knows" something. They do not make generalizations about women who have intuition. But, both men and women have intuition. It is not talked about, nor is it called psychic ability. Recall, intuition can be defined as the human soul's quality to consciously or unconsciously receive thought information beyond the limitations of the mind.

Understanding what you know and how you know things is a big part of being able to develop your gifts. Identifying your abilities is helpful, and the foundation of your development starts within you with your willingness to look and see, hear and listen, and speak and be heard. Above all, you need to practice diligence and patience in order to improve yourself.

Exercise

Recall an instance when you or someone you know said that their intuition was the reason that they had an answer to a problem or knew about something in advance.

_____

_____

This was a time when intuition or one of your other psychic senses was at work. There may not be an understanding of which psychic ability created the *knowing*, but all of them help with understanding situations not easily explained with the logical mind.

BODY LANGUAGE

Psychic Minute Fifty

Body language and other signals spur our intuition.

When you meet people and notice their body language, they are sending you silent signals that your intuition interprets. The way a person stands, uses their eyes, or sits can be an indication of their mood or their motive when you meet them. Observing your reaction to the person will help you assess an encounter. In order to use your intuition properly, you should accept that the information you "just know" is essential and important.

Soul Exercise

Recall an instance when a person's body language indicated a hidden agenda.

_____

_____

This is another instance when your intuition can be a very valuable tool to have at your disposal. Recognizing the signals your body is sending to you or the thoughts that drop into your mind may be the clues that save you from making a bad decision. Once you have trusted that sudden awareness from another person's body language, you can exert wise caution.

This use of intuition can also be used while driving your car. At some time, you have probably "just known" when another driver was going to pull out in front of you. By paying attention to your intuition, you may have avoided a disaster. However, intuition may not be the only psychic sense warning you to be aware of the person next to you. We need to reiterate that the psychic senses often work together. While it is important to define them singularly, they often mesh together leaving it difficult to discuss them separately. You may have a feeling (clairsentience), see a vision (clairvoyance), or hear a sound (clairaudience) that serves as a warning to you as well.

INTUITION SELF-EXAMINATION

Psychic Minute Fifty-One

Self-examination of your intuitive abilities involves remembering moments in your past when your thoughts provided an answer or revelation.

Developing your intuitive skills includes reviewing your experiences. Here are some questions you can ask yourself.

Soul Exercise

1. Do you just know the answer to some problems without any provocation?

   _____

2. Does accurate information come to you about a person with a first impression?

   _____

3. Do you sense answers are just "dropped" into your mind?

   _____

4. Do you receive answers that allow you to feel, see, or hear other impressions about a situation?

   _____

5. Do you notice that you do not act upon a situation until you "just know" what to do?

   _____

6. Do you notice that you use the phrase "I know" when evaluating a situation?

   _____

7. Please describe an experience when you used your ability to "just know" to help you in a particular instance.

   _____

INTUITION WORKS WITH OTHER PSYCHIC SENSES

Psychic Minute Fifty-Two

Intuition works interchangeably with your other psychic abilities.

It is often the first psychic sense we accept, and then other abilities are noticed. For example, we may have an intuitive thought and immediately receive feelings, visions, smells, tastes, or words to support the intuitive impression.

Clairaudience is commonly used with intuition. We often hear an inner voice providing us with specific information to solve a problem or assisting us in determining our life's mission. Listening and accepting information can be difficult because it often interferes with logical impressions we receive from our physical senses.

Soul Exercise

Recall an instance when you had a psychic thought and then noticed other reactions followed.

_____

_____

INTUITION AND THE LOGICAL MIND

Psychic Minute Fifty-Three

Learning to trust your intuition is often difficult because your logical mind may convince you that your impression is false.

However, intuition assists us in problem-solving and discovering our life's path. Following your intuition allows for insight into your abilities and assists you in pursuing successful results. *Peace of mind is the result when we learn to balance our intuition and our logical thoughts.*

TOOLS FOR DEVELOPMENT

Psychic Minute Fifty-Four

There are several tools and techniques you can use to assist you in developing your intuition.

Journaling

This practice is instrumental with helping you develop all of your psychic abilities and discover the way the energy of your soul works. It is good to keep a record over a period of time of your responses and the way you handled similar experiences. Journaling allows you to gain perspective of yourself. It is this perspective that will allow you to be most effective in your life and to live your life with fulfillment.

Recognition of sudden and unexpected thoughts

Recognizing intuition and when ideas and thoughts just drop into your mind is a healthy exercise. Noticing when you have hunches and when you just know that you are right allows you to learn to trust yourself and gain confidence in your psychic abilities.

Frequent napping

Napping for a short time during the day has many benefits including improving your physical well-being. Using napping as a tool to enhance intuition is best used when attempting to solve a problem. Often, when you "sleep on it", answers suddenly appear. While napping is not 100% of problem solving, it can assist you in developing your intuitive skills. Fifteen minute catnaps can be very effective in giving you peace of mind when dealing with nagging problems that do not have easy solutions. Taking a break from these issues can leave you open to allowing the answers to come to you. Also, taking a walk or finding another type of diversion can assist you in removing mental blocks. This is especially good for creative types.

Mind Games

Games such as puzzles, jumble, and charades can assist you in recognizing and developing your intuition. These games allow you to sense when an idea simply "drops" into your mind. This sensation may feel odd at first, but once you understand that this is intuition, you will recognize it when it occurs in your everyday life.

Meditation

Meditation is a tool for the development of all of your psychic abilities and can be used very effectively to develop intuition. Creating time and a place for meditation is essential for it to be successful for you. Quieting your mind allows you to detach and observe using your psychic abilities without the assistance of your physical senses.

Here are some tips for effective meditation:

1. Create time in your schedule to meditate on a regular basis.
2. Find a suitable quiet place, with a comfortable temperature, proper lighting, and a peaceful atmosphere.
3. Set your intention.
4. Relax your body and mind by either being quiet, listening to music or a meditation recording, or using some other technique to clear your mind and leave behind your daily activities.

5. Allow yourself to acquire information from your feelings, from your visions, by listening for guidance, or by just knowing answers.

6. Once you have obtained information, you can resume your normal activities feeling refreshed and at peace.

Take a break

When working on a problem causing considerable angst, it is often a good idea to just take a break. A short walk or another distraction can be a very helpful with problem solving. The time away allows your intuition to function unencumbered by your conscious mind. Answers are not guaranteed, but there is a greater chance of success as you are relieving some of the pressure you have put on yourself. This allows answers to flow more freely.

Review

Reread this chapter and dwell on the points that make the most sense to you. You will find you have had many more intuitive experiences than you originally thought. It is more than coincidence that ideas just come to you. It is intuition, and the energy of your soul at work.

CHAPTER ELEVEN

CONNECTING WITH SPIRIT AND PSYCHIC ABILITIES

During the development of your psychic abilities, you will encounter more than just psychic impressions. You will experience the sensations of entities beyond our physical world. It is natural to have angels, guides, and loved ones around you. With further inspection, you will notice animals and other entities visiting from other places. They make life experiences more interesting and can give you insights that you may not have thought possible.

This chapter briefly explores the further development of your psychic senses incorporating mediumship as a natural progression for them. A more intense discussion is necessary to fully explore connecting with spirit, and it is a topic for another time and another book.

Introduction

The bond between people is spiritual, and this spiritual bond is what allows sensations to be sent to you. Physical distances do not matter when the extended senses are activated, and this is true for the dimensions as well. You sense the presence of people you have known after they have crossed-over into the next dimension. The ability to detect spirit is comforting since it validates the idea that we continue after we have left the physical plane. Most of us have some belief about what happens to us when we leave our physical bodies. Regardless of whether or not your belief system supports notions such as heaven and hell, you can sense whether or not a spirit is at peace. The religious concepts are judgment calls for others to make. However, the peace that you are able to sense from a person in the spirit world indicates a kind of heaven, while their lack of peace indicates a kind of hell.

The idea of communicating with spirits, mediumship, is the most controversial of all of metaphysical topics, but interest in exploring this possibility is growing. Our society sends strong signals about mediumship being a forbidden activity because the Bible clearly states that we should stay away from spirits. This stigma invokes a great deal of fear of people who are able to connect with those in spirit. Not only is there the idea that it is wrong, but it can even be associated with mental illness. As a result, we have the tendency to keep these experiences to ourselves at the risk of being labeled as 'crazy'. Since a certain amount of courage is needed to discuss spirit visitations, we often reserve these types of topics for discussions with like-minded individuals, open to the idea of communicating with people or entities in the spirit world. Mediumship is primarily focused on loved ones, and most of the spirits that we encounter are good. However, there are rare occurrences when people come in contact with 'evil' spirits. While evil spirits do exist, they are more often found in the imagination and in movies that highlight beings with supernatural powers, such as vampires and werewolves. These stories allow us to be scared but are not taken very seriously by credible people working with psychic ability.

Psychic Minute Fifty-Five

Mediumship is the ability of the human soul to sense the presence of another life force beyond our physical presence.

This means that you can sense another entity with any of your psychic senses. Each of the psychic senses has been discussed in previous chapters, and now that information is incorporated in this one. You can use your personal space as a vehicle, allowing you to read and interpret energy surrounding other individuals. You can sense the soul of a person in the living by their energy level, for a person who is in their physical form projects a higher level of energy than a person who has crossed-over.

DIFFERENCE BETWEEN A PSYCHIC AND A MEDIUM

Psychic Minute Fifty-Six

The difference between psychic ability and the ability to connect with spirit lies in the kind of energy received around the client. Psychic energy deals with information and events concerning a client; whereas, a medium connects with the energy of a spirit around a client.

It is important to note this difference between psychic ability and mediumship. A medium discerns information about the spirit's relationship with the client and the events the spirit reveals. It should also be noted that a spirit chooses whether or not to appear, and it gives only the information it wants to share with the medium.

> *Personal Experience:*
> *When I see something, I explain it the best that I can. However, if I am told I am wrong, I analyze what I saw and then learn from the client. I learn from what they told me about the correct information. It makes me a better psychic and medium. It would make no sense for me to argue with someone about a situation I did not explain properly.*
> *A recent Circle of Healing and Enlightenment is a good example. I do 'Circles' in the dark, so I have no way of physically seeing from where the information is*

coming. I do not allow the clients to tell me anything because they are there to receive not to give.

On this particular night, I had nine people in my Circle. I made major hits on eight of the nine people in the room. They acted as if they were astonished at the information I gave them, but one lady disagreed. She said I hit nothing, and she was not going to provide me with any clarification. I could not disagree with her because I had never met her, and if she said I was wrong then I was wrong. I could not let it get to me because I had already received validation from eight others. My confidence is rarely shaken these days.

The first impression I gave her was about a man in spirit. I saw that this man was close to her, but he did not give me an indication as to who he was at first glance. I thought he was a husband, brother, or close friend. There was a bond or a 'love' interest there. It was clear. She said she did not have anyone like that in spirit around her. She said she was surprised that no one else showed up. I then told her about her parents and gave her accurate descriptions of both of them. She did acknowledge their personalities with a minimal amount of resistance. I believe, in her mind, she was being fair.

When you are in this type of situation, the energy in the room goes a little haywire. It is not pleasant when there is resistance to your readings, especially when there is so much validation by others.

At the end of the reading with the lady, she said that she had wanted her son to come in. She said that since he was not a husband, brother, or a love interest, the man was not him. He was 25 years old when he died in the army, but this was not information I received from him. The man simply showed up and demonstrated he was a happy go lucky person and loved her.

I can only give the information that comes and cannot worry about it. The reason I am sharing this with you is because I do not want you to lose confidence if the information you receive is not exact. Psychic ability revolves around the 'edges' of information, and the best psychics in the world work with these edges. We have to use our cognitive abilities to get the rest of the picture.

DIFFERENT TYPES OF MEDIUMS

Psychic Minute Fifty-Seven

There are at least two different types of mediums connecting with spirits: trance mediums and evidential mediums.

Trance mediums are very connected to the spirits with which they are working. You may see changes in their physical appearance or voice. A trance medium is a channel and allows a spirit to have at least partial control of their body. The most famous of this type of medium is Edgar Cayce.

Evidential mediums communicate information they receive from spirits. They may or may not remember this information after a session is completed. Most mediums are evidential mediums, and they are the focus of this chapter.

Multiple Dimensions

You will find that there are many types of spirits trying to communicate with you, and noticing a spirit is only the first aspect of mediumship. Through experience, you will understand that life forces exude different frequencies and sensations that will in turn resonate differently with you. You must realize that energy comes from multiple dimensions and learn how to distinguish it, for this is a nuance of mediumship.

Psychic Minute Fifty-Eight

There are different types of spirits who connect with us. They visit us from another dimension and come from different areas I call "A" fields.

Spirits from other dimensions include: our ancestors, angels and guides, animal spirits, aliens (extraterrestrials), "ghosts", elementals, and any spirit considered a "demon". Paranormal spirits, our ancestors, friends and loved ones, animal spirits, and "ghosts" are all in the same dimensional category since they have all lived on Earth at some point. However, angels and guides have a different frequency from other spirits. They may or may not have previously lived in this dimension, but they do show themselves to us. Some people argue that guides once lived on Earth and angels never have, but there are different schools of thought on the subject depending upon a person's belief system. Demons are fallen angels, have made the choice not to follow God, and suffer from their decisions. While their decisions were made freely, they are final and cannot be reversed. Extraterrestrials are the most controversial category for most people. You may or may not have seen them from another dimension, but some people have seen them on this physical plane. The one's you see with your mind's eye do not have a spacecraft. Extraterrestrials can be a topic all of their own because they vibrate with completely different energy from the spirits you usually see.

Psychic Minute Fifty-Nine

The simplest method of connecting with spirit is to visualize a person in spirit, such as a loved one or friend, and dwell on their energy.

You can begin by asking God for protection while working with spirits since there is no need to desire or attract anything negative to come to you in this process. Meditating and asking the spirit to come to you in a positive manner is a good practice. Ask them to give you clear and concise information to demonstrate that it is truly them coming to you from the spirit world. During the course of this book, you have used your personal space to exercise your psychic ability, and now you are using it as a way to sense spirit around you. By expanding your personal space, you are able to capture the energy of a spirit.

All of the psychic senses have an element of mediumship to them because you sense a presence using any one or all of them. For example, you can feel, see, hear, or know a spirit is around you. Some spirits show their presence with a familiar fragrance or even the taste of a favorite meal. It depends upon the spirit and the manner in which they wish to communicate. We retain our freedom of choice when we pass away. Spirits decide whether or not they wish to communicate, but it is up to us to sense them when they do.

Use your abilities to tune into their energy. Remember the way you felt when you were with them. What are you seeing, hearing, feeling, knowing about the person in spirit? This exercise can be done with angels, guides, aliens, and animals as well.

As you begin to learn to be a medium, you may notice that you have unusual physical symptoms such as yawning or twitching. Some people may cough or even sneeze when they are in the presence of a spirit. Over time, you will recognize that a spirit is coming in when you start having one of these sensations.

Mediumship has a physical aspect to it because there are times when your physical senses detect spirits around you. For instance, when you see a spirit, usually out of the corners of your eyes, you may call them "ghosts". A voice coming out of nowhere is called a "direct voice". Hearing a voice other than your inner voice can be a form of connecting with a spirit.

Psychic Minute Sixty

Spirits can be detected through any of the psychic senses.
You can feel, see, hear, smell, taste or just know the presence of a spirit.

Using Your Mind's Eye

When you see spirits around others using your mind's eye, they often appear in certain positions around people. For me, a father in spirit often shows himself over the right shoulder. Fathers appear close to a person, and grandfathers are above and just behind the father. Mothers appear over the left shoulder, and grandmothers appear above and just behind them. Other ancestors may appear above the grandparent position. Husbands, wives, siblings, or other contemporaries are on the right or left side of the shoulder depending upon the sex. Men are usually on the right, and women are on the left. The exception to this is maternal or paternal grandparents. They may appear on the mother or father's side even though they are both male and female. Children are usually in front of a person. Angels and Guides appear behind a person, and animals are in front or at the feet.

These parameters may or may not be true for you, but they can serve as a guide. Everyone is different, and it needs to be reiterated that development of your abilities is an individual endeavor. Our experiences can be similar in many areas while unique in others.

Spirits Bringing Other Spirits

There are times when one spirit will bring another to join them. The initial contacting spirit opens the pathway for others to make their presence known. For example, a grandfather may appear first, only to have the grandmother take over the communicating once she has arrived.

Dreaming About a Spirit or a Person

Finally, spirits can come to you during your dreams or during an astral projection. You may have an "out of body" connection with someone on the other side when they want to communicate a special message or visit with you.

Recognizing the Information Given to You from Spirit

We have just discussed sensing spirits with your psychic ability and the placement of spirits when they appear around you. Now, we are going to move on to describing the types of information that they communicate.

The Death Experience - The moment of death is often described by the person in spirit. They can tell you who was in the room with them when they died, the moment they left their body, and the people and guides that assisted them in crossing over to the next realm.

Soul Meditation

Go to your sacred space and call upon your loved ones and guides to give you evidence of their presence. When you begin to meditate, be sure to surround yourself with white light and ask for protection from any negative energy. Ask for positive information and spirits to be present around you. Be sensitive to your extended senses and the information you are receiving.

Review

Practice surrounding yourself with white light and protecting your session with spirit. Use your psychic senses to develop insight and understanding.

CHAPTER TWELVE

AN HOUR OF PSYCHIC MINUTES

Psychic Minute One

We exercise our souls by examining our past experiences, paying attention to sensations and impressions from beyond the physical, and practicing.

Psychic Minute Two

The energy of your soul captures energy from the Divine and sends energy that can be interpreted.

Psychic Minute Three

Psychic ability 1) provides you with an early warning system to prevent you from being in danger, 2) validates or does not validate impressions you receive from your physical senses, 3) gives perspective, and 4) allows you to create. It is the energy of inspiration!

Psychic Minute Four

The way you understand your innate abilities helps you learn about your strongest psychic skill.

Psychic Minute Five

There are two sides of psychic energy. The energies of sending and receiving energy are equal.

Psychic Minute Six

Practice and validation are important assets to have when learning to use your abilities.

Psychic Minute Seven

A journal chronicling experiences will help you with your psychic profile and validate your skills.

Psychic Minute Eight

Most people are drawn to metaphysics through a trauma, an event, or a curiosity that causes them to examine their belief systems and/or explore their personal abilities.

Psychic Minute Nine

The study of metaphysics and/or psychic ability by individuals is a "journey of self-discovery".

Psychic Minute Ten

Metaphysics is the study of existence "beyond the physical".

Psychic Minute Eleven

Developing psychic skills involves discovering a personal profile of abilities.

Psychic Minute Twelve

We access our psychic abilities by using "extensions" of our physical senses.

Psychic Minute Thirteen

The primary mechanism to access your psychic abilities is meditation.

Psychic Minute Fourteen

Clairsentience is the soul's capacity to capture "feelings" or emotional information beyond the physical limitations of the nervous system.

Psychic Minute Fifteen

Psychic touch, also known as clairtangency or psychometry, is the soul's capacity to use a physical experience to capture information "beyond the physical" from people, objects, and/or animals.

Psychic Minute Sixteen

Clairvoyance, or "clear vision", is the voluntary and/or involuntary ability of the human soul to access visual information solely within the mind, and it can happen suddenly and without warning.

Psychic Minute Seventeen

Clairaudience is the soul's capacity to capture audio information beyond the physical limits of the ears.

Psychic Minute Eighteen

Clairgustance is the recognition of a particular taste sensation in your mouth without any explanation of the origin.

Psychic Minute Nineteen

Clairfragrance is the human quality to capture scents beyond the physical limitations of the olfactory glands.

Psychic Minute Twenty

Intuition, claircognizance, is the soul's capacity to receive "ideas" from beyond the limitations of the mind.

Psychic Minute Twenty-One

Clairsentience is the soul's ability to consciously and/or unconsciously capture "feeling" or emotional information beyond the limitations of your physical nervous system.

Psychic Minute Twenty-Two

Sudden feelings are usually associated with imminent danger or immediate action.

Psychic Minute Twenty-Three

Empathy is a physical response sensing the emotions of another person.

Psychic Minute Twenty-Four

Sympathy pains are actual pains we may experience when we are aware of another person's health condition.

Psychic Minute Twenty-Five

Humans are physical and spiritual beings who emit and receive energy.

Psychic Minute Twenty-Six

An energy imprint is a residual impression of life experiences from a person which is left on another person, place, object, or living thing (i.e. an animal).

Psychic Minute Twenty-Seven

A sound imprint is an energy imprint created by a person, animal, or event revealing reality beyond the physical limits of our human hearing.

Psychic Minute Twenty-Eight

Psychic information is most valuable when it can be independently verified.

Psychic Minute Twenty-Nine

Imprinted energy emits a low frequency we can detect and follow with our psychic senses.

Psychic Minute Thirty

Psychic touch, or psychometry, requires a clear mind and the self-knowledge concerning your ability to capture energy.

Psychic Minute Thirty-One

The mind's eye is located above the eyebrows in the middle of the forehead. This is the area where your soul's vision resides, and it is not associated with your physical vision.

Psychic Minute Thirty-Two

The human aura is the electromagnetic field which surrounds the body. The auric field can be sensed by our soul's abilities, and some claim it can be photographed by an aura camera.

Psychic Minute Thirty-Three

Remote viewing is the ability to identify information or an object by focusing your clairvoyance on a distant and/or specific location.

Psychic Minute Thirty-Four

We experience many different kinds of dreams. While a few dreams seem to be only fragments of memories, images, or nonsensical episodes, most dreams have some psychic element to them.

Psychic Minute Thirty-Five

Dreams occur during periods when the mind is distracted or in a sleep state. They can be the result of the imagination or the brain's natural ability to process information. Dreams are a collection of feelings, images, symbols and/or events. There are several types of dreams, and each has unique aspects.

Psychic Minute Thirty-Six

Psychic abilities are a special part of the human experience, and dreams can help you with your discovery of them. Dreams give you special insight into the ability of your soul to help you overcome issues and are part of your psychic journey to understand life.

Psychic Minute Thirty-Seven

Using the soul's ability to capture words or advice is called a "mantra".

Psychic Minute Thirty-Eight

As with the other psychic senses, clairaudience has nuances associated with it. These include active prayer, "direct voice", and hearing the thoughts of another person.

Psychic Minute Thirty-Nine

Clairgustance should not be confused with a heightened sense of taste.

Psychic Minute Forty

Psychic taste can enable you to recognize a spirit around you.

Psychic Minute Forty-One

It is often noted that the psychic sense of smell and taste are used together as one. Furthermore, it works with your other psychic senses to alert you.

Psychic Minute Forty-Two

Psychic smell can make you aware of a spirit around you.

Psychic Minute Forty-Three

You may become more aware of your surroundings from your psychic sense of smell.

Psychic Minute Forty-Four

Clairfragrance should not be confused with a heightened sense of smell.

Psychic Minute Forty-Five

As with the other psychic senses, psychic smell also has remote components.

Psychic Minute Forty-Six

Learning to use your psychic ability is not a competition.

Psychic Minute Forty-Seven

The mechanism of intuition is derived from the energy of the soul.

Psychic Minute Forty-Eight

The use of the gift of intuition is used by the most intelligent people thus creating a Genius Theory.

Psychic Minute Forty-Nine

The expression, women's intuition, is a term commonly used by our society to acknowledge the uncanny accuracy of many women to innately have answers to problems or to make predictions.

Psychic Minute Fifty

Body language and other signals spur our intuition.

Psychic Minute Fifty-One

Self-examination of your intuitive abilities involves remembering moments in your past when your thoughts provided an answer or revelation.

Psychic Minute Fifty-Two

Intuition works interchangeably with your other psychic abilities.

Psychic Minute Fifty-Three

Learning to trust your intuition is often difficult because your logical mind may convince you that your impression is false.

Psychic Minute Fifty-Four

There are several tools and techniques you can use to assist you in developing your intuition.

The following "Psychic Minutes" are associated with the concepts in the next workbook series, <u>Sitting with Spirit</u>.

Psychic Minute Fifty-Five

Mediumship is the ability of the human soul to sense the presence of another life force beyond our physical presence.

Psychic Minute Fifty-Six

The difference between psychic ability and the ability to connect with spirit lies in the kind of energy received around the client. Psychic energy deals with information and events concerning a client; whereas, a medium connects with the energy of a spirit around a client.

Psychic Minute Fifty-Seven

There are at least two different types of mediums connecting with spirits: trance mediums and evidential mediums.

Psychic Minute Fifty-Eight

There are different types of spirits who connect with us. They visit us from another dimension and come from different areas I call "A" fields.

Psychic Minute Fifty-Nine

The simplest method of connecting with spirit is to visualize a person in spirit, such as a loved one or friend, and dwell on their energy.

Psychic Minute Sixty

Spirits can be detected through any of the psychic senses.

CONCLUSION

This book ends by returning to the beginning and stating that *one of mankind's greatest gifts from the Divine is psychic ability.* Learn all you can from others and develop your own techniques. Remember to practice by observing other psychics, receiving readings, and giving them to others. It will serve you well. It takes time and patience to develop these natural gifts that we all have. Use them wisely, and they will enrich your life. Your journey begins..............

Printed in the United States
By Bookmasters